# DE
# SPIRITUS ANGELUS

# PSEUDOMONARCHIA

# DÆMONUM

---

# DE SEPTEM SECUNDEIS

---

# DÆMONOLOGIE

# CONTENTS

## PSEUDOMONARCHIA DÆMONUM

### LECTORIS(Latin)

### PSEUDOMONARCHIA DÆMONUM (Latin)

### PSEUDOMONARCHIA DÆMONUM (English)

### READER (English)

#### CHAPTER III
The houres wherin principall divels may be bound, to wit, raised and restrained from dooing of hurt.

#### CHAPTER IV
The forme of adjuring or citing of the spirits aforesaid to arise and appeare

# DE SEPTEM SECUNDEIS

**DEDICATION**

**DE SEPTEM SECUNDEIS**

**THE FUTURE SERIES OF THIS REVOLUTION REQUIRES PROPHECY**


# DÆMONOLOGIE

**INTRODUCTION**

**PREFACE**

**THE FIRST BOOKE**
Daemonologie, in Forme of ane Dialogue

CHAPTER I
CHAPTER II
CHAPTER III
CHAPTER IIII
CHAPTER V
CHAPTER VI
CHAPTER VII

**THE SECONDE BOOKE**
Of Dæmonologie Argvment. The description of Sorcerie an Witch-craft in speciall.

CHAPTER I
CHAPTER II
CHAPTER III
CHAPTER IIII
CHAPTER V
CHAPTER VI

**CHAPTER VII**

**THE THIRDE BOOKE**
Of Dæmonologie Argvment. The description of all these kindes of Spirites that troubles men or women. The conclusion of the whole Dialogue.

**CHAPTER I**
**CHAPTER II**
**CHAPTER III**
**CHAPTER IIII**
**CHAPTER V**
**CHAPTER VI**

# PSEUDOMONARCHIA DÆMONIUM

# PSEUDOMONARCHIA DÆMONUM

**JOHANN WEYER**

*"O curas hominum, ô quantum est in rebus inane?"*

-- C. Lucilius, Satires of Persius

## LECTORIS

Ne Sathanicæ factionis monopolium usqueadeo porro delitescat, hanc Dæmonum Pseudomonarchiam, ex Acharonticorum Vasallorum archivo subtractam, in hujus Operis de Dæmonum præstigiis calce annectere volui, ut effascinatorum id genus hominum, qui se magos jactitare non erubescunt, curiositas, præstigiæ, vanitas, dolus, imposturæ, deliria, mens elusa, & manifesta mendacia, quinimo non ferendæ blasphemiæ, omnium mortalium, qui in mediæ lucis splendore hallucinari nolint, oculis clarissimè appareant, hoc potissimum seculo scelestissimo, quo Christi regnum tam enormi impunitaque tyrannide impetitur ab iis qui Beliali palàm sacramentum præstitêre, stipendium etiam justum hauddubie recepturi: quibus & perditas has horas libenter dedico, si forte ex immensa Dei misericordia convertantur & vivant: quod ex animo iis precor, sitque felix & faustum. Ne autem curiosulus aliquis, fascino nimis detentus, hoc stultitiæ argumentum temere imitari audeat, voces hinc inde prætermisi studio, ut universa delinquendi occasio præcideretur. Inscribitur vero à maleferiato hoc hominum genere Officium spirituum, vel, Liber officiorum spirituum, seu, Liber dictus Empto. Salomonis, de principibus & regibus dæmoniorum, qui cogi possunt divina virtute & humana. At mihi nuncupabitur Pseudomonarchia Dæmonum.

## PSEUDOMONARCHIA DÆMONUM

*(1) Primus Rex, qui est de potestate Orientis, dicitur Baël, apparens tribus capitibus, quorum unum assimilatur bufoni alterum homini, tertium feli. Rauca loquitur voce, formator morum & insignis certator, reddit hominem invisibilem & sapientem. Huic obediunt sexagintasex legiones.*

*(2) Agares Dux primus sub potestate Orientis, apparet benevolus in senioris hominis forma, equitans in crocodilo, & in manu accipitrem portans. Cuncta linguarum genera docet optime: fugitantes reverti facit, & permanentes fugere: prælaturas & dignitates dimittit, & tripudiare facit spiritus terræ: & est de ordine Virtutum, sub sua potestate habens triginta & unam legiones.*

*(3) Marbas, alias Barbas, Præses magnus, se manifestans in fortissimi leonis specie, sed ab exorcista accitus humana induitur forma, & de occultis plene respondet, morbos invehit & tollit, promovet sapientiam artiumque mechanicarum cognitionem, homines adhæc in aliam mutat formã. Præest trigintasex legionibus.*

*(4) Pruflas, alibi invenitur Bufas, magnus Princeps & Dux est, cujus mansio circa turrim Babylonis, & videtur in eo flamma foris, caput autem assimilatur magno nycticoraci. Autor est*

& promotor discordiarum, bellorum, rixarum & mendaciorum. Omnibus in locis non intromittatur. Ad quæsita respondet abunde. Sub sunt huic legiones vinginti sex, partim ex ordine Throni, partim Angelorum.

(5) Amon vel Aamon Marchio magnus & potens, prodit in lupi forma caudam habens serpentinam, & flammam evomens. Hominis autem indutus speciem, caninos ostentat dentes, & caput magno nycticoraci simile. Princeps omnium fortissimus est, intelligens præterita & futura, hinc & gratiam concilians omnium amicorum & inimicorum. Quadraginta imperat legionibus.

(6) Barbatos magnus Comes & Dux, apparet in signo Sagittarii silvestris cum quatuor regibus tubas ferentibus. Intelligit cantus avium, canum latratus, mugitus boum & cunctorum animalium: thesauros item à magis & incantatoribus reconditos, detegit: Et est ex ordine Virtutum, partim Dominationum. Triginta præsidet legionibus. Novit præterita & futura: tam amicorum quam inimicorum animos conciliat.

(7) Buer Præses magnus conspicitur in signo *. Absolute docet philosophiam, practicam, ethica item & logica, & herbarum vires: Dat optimos familiares: Ægros sanitati restituere novit, maxime & homines. Quinquaginta legionum habet imperium.

(8) Gusoyn Dux magnus & fortis, apparet in forma zenophali. Explicate respondet & vere de præsentibus, præteritis, futuris & occultis. Amicoram & inimicorum gratiam reddit: Dignitates confert & honores conformat. Præest quadragintaquinque legionibus.

(9) Botis, alibi Otis, magnus Præses & Comes, Prodit in viperæ specie deterrima: Et siquando formam induit humanam dentes ostendit magnos & cornua duo, manu

*gladium acutum portans. Dat perfecte responsa vera de præsentius, præteritis, futuris & abstrusis. Tam amicos quam hostes conciliat. Sexaginta imperat legionibus.*

*(10) Bathym, alibi Marthim Dux magnus & fortis: Visitur constitutione viri fortissimi cum cauda serpentina, equo pallido insidens. Virtutes herbarum & lapidum pretiosorum intelligit. Cursu velocissimo hominem de regione in regionem transfert. Huic triginta subsunt legiones.*

*(11) Pursan, alias Curson, magnus Rex, prodit ut homo facie leonina, viperam portans ferocissimam, ursoque insidens, quem semper præcedunt tubæ. Callet præsentia, præterita & futura: Aperit occulta, thesauros detegit: Corpus humanum suscipit & aëreum. Vere respondet de rebus terrenis & occultis, de divinitate & mundi creatione: Familiares parit optimos: Cui parent vigintiduo legiones, partim de ordine Virtutum, partim ex ordine Throni.*

*(12) Eligor, alias Abigor, Dux magnus, apparet ut miles pulcherrimus, lanceam, vexillum & sceptrum portans. Plene de occultis respondet atque bellis, & quomodo milites occurrere debeant: Futura scit, & gratiam apud omnes dominos & milites conciliat. Præsidet sexaginta legionibus.*

*(13) Loray, alias Oray, magnus Marchio, se ostendens in forma sagittarii pulcherrimi, pharetram & arcum gestantis: author existit omnium præliorum, & vulnera putrefacit quæ à sagittariis infliguntur, quos objicit optimos tribus diebus. Triginta dominatur legionibus.*

*(14) Valefar, alias Malaphar, Dux est fortis, forma leonis prodiens & capite latronis. Familiaritatem parit suis, donec laqueo suspendantur. Decem præsidet legionibus.*

*(15) Morax, alias Foraii, magnus Comes & Præses: Similis tauro visitur: Et si quando humanam faciem assumit,*

*admirabilem in Astronomia & in omnibus artibus liberalibus reddit hominem: parit etiam famulos non malos & sapientes: novit & herbarum & pretiosorum lapidum potentiam. Imperat triginta sex legionibus.*

*(16) Ipes, alias Ayperos est magnus Comes & Princeps, apparens quidem specie angelica, interim leone obscurior & turpis, capite leonis, pedibus anserinis, cauda leporina. Præterita & futura novit: Redditque hominem ingeniosum & audacem. Legiones huic obediunt trigintasex.*

*(17) Naberus, alias Cerberus, Marchio est fortis, forma corvi se ostentans: Si quando loquitur, raucam edit vocem. Reddit & hominem amabilem & artium intelligentem, cum primis in Rhetoricis eximium. Prælaturarum & dignitatum jacturam parit. Novendecim legiones hunc audiunt.*

*(18) Glasya labolas, alias Caacrinolaas vel Caassimolar magnus Præses: Qui progreditur ut canis habens alas gryphi. Artium cognitionem dat, interim dux omnium homicidarum. Præsentia & futura intelligit. Tam amicorum quam inimicorum animos demeretur: Et hominem reddit invisibilem. Imperium habet triginta sex legionum.*

*(19) Zepar Dux magnus, apparens uti miles, inflammansque virorum amore mulieres, & quando ipsi jussum fuerit, earum formam in aliam transmutat, donec dilectis suis fruantur. Steriles quoque eas facit. Vigintisex huic parent legiones.*

*(20) Byleth Rex magnus & terribilis, in equo pallido equitans, quem præcedunt tubæ, symphoniæ, & cuncta Musicæ genera. Quum autem coram exorcista se ostentat, turgidus ira & furore videtur, ut decipiat. Exorcista vero tum sibi prudenter caveat: Atque ut fastum ei adimat, in manu suscipiat baculum corili, cum quo orientem & meridiem versus, foris juxta circulum manum extendet, facietque triangulum. Cæterum si manum non extendit, & intrare jubet, atque*

*spirituum Vinculum ille renuerit, ad lectionem progrediatur exorcista: mox ingredietur item submissus, ibi stando & faciendo quodcunque jufferit exorcista ipsi Byleth regi, eritque securus. Si vero contumacior fuerit, nec primo jussu circulum ingredi voluerit, reddetur forte timidior exorcista: Vel si Vinculum spirituum minus habuerit, sciet haud dubie exorcista, malignos spiritus postea eum non verituros, at semper viliorem habituros. Item si ineptior sit locus triangulo deducendo juxta circulum, tunc vas vino plenum ponatur: Et intelliget exorcista certissimè, quum è domo sua egressus fuerit cum sociis suis, prædictum Byleth sibi fautorem fore, benevolum, & coram ipso submissum quando progredietur. Venientem vero exorcista benigne suscipiat, & de ipsius fastu glorietur: Propterea quoque eundem adorabit, quemadmodum alii reges, quia nihil dicit absque aliis principibus. Item si hic Byleth accitus fuerit ab aliquo exorcista, semper tenendus ad exorcistæ faciem annulus argenteus medii digiti manus sinistræ, quemadmodum pro Amaymone. Nec est prætermittenda dominatio & potestas tanti principis, quoniam nullus est sub potestate & dominatione exorcistæ alius, qui viros & mulieres in delirio detinet, donec exorcistæ voluntatem explerint: Et fuit ex ordine Potestatum, sperans se ad septimum Thronum rediturum, quod minus credibile. Imperat octogintaquinque legionibus.*

*(21) Sytry, alias Bitru, magnus Princeps, leopardi facie apparens, habensque alas velut gryphi. Quando autem humanam assumit formam, mire pulcher videtur. Incendit virum mulieris amore, mulierem vicissim alterius desiderio incitat. Jussus secreta libenter detegit feminarum, eas ridens ludificansque, ut se luxuriose nudent. Huic sexaginta legiones obsequuntur.*

*(22) Paymon obedit magis Lucifero quam alii reges. Lucifer hic intelligendus, qui in profunditate scientiæ suæ demersus, Deo assimilari voluit, & ob hanc arrogantiam in exitium*

*projectus est. De quo dictum est: Omnis lapis pretiosus operimentum tuum Ezech. 28 . Paymon autem cogitur virtute divina, ut se sistat coram exorcista: ubi hominis induit simulachrum, insidens dromedario, coronaque insignitus lucidissima, & vultu fœmineo. Hunc præcedit exercitus cum tubis & cimbalis bene sonantibus, atque omnibus instrumentis Musicis, primo cum ingenti clamore & rugitu apparens, sicut in Empto. Salomonis, & arte declaratur. Et si Paymon hic quandoque loquitur, ut minus ab exorcista intelligatur, propterea is non tepescat: sed ubi porrexerit illi primam chartam ut voto suo obsequatur, jubebit quoque ut distincte & aperte respondeat ad quæsita, & de universa philosophia & prudentia vel scientia, & de cæteris arcanis. Et si voles cognoscere dispositionem mundi, & qualis sit terra, aut quid eam fustineat in aqua, aut aliquid aliud, & quid sit abyssus, & ubi est ventus & unde veniat, abunde te docebit. Accedant & consecrationes tam de libationibus quam aliis. Confert hic dignitates & confirmationes. Resistentes sibi suo vinculo deprimit, & exorcistæ subjicit. Bonos comparat famulos, & artium omnium intellectum. Notandum, quod in advocando hunc Paymonem, Aquilonem versus exorcistam conspicere oporteat, quæ ibi hujus sit hospitium. Accitum vero intrepide constanterque suscipiat, interroget, & ab eo petat quicquid voluerit, nec dubie impetrabit. At ne creatorem oblivioni tradat, cavendum exorcistæ, propter ea quæ præmissa fuerunt de Paymone. Sunt qui dicunt, eum ex ordine Dominationum fuisse: sed aliis placet, ex ordine Cherubin. Hunc sequuntur legiones ducentæ, partim ex ordine Angelorum, partim Potestatum. Notandum adhæc, si Paymon solus fuerit citatus per aliquam libationem aut sacrificium, duo reges magni comitantur, scilicet Bebal & Abalam, & alii potentes. In hujus exercitu sunt vigintiquinque legiones: Quia spiritus his subjecti, non semper ipsis adsunt, nisi ut appareant, divina virtute compellantur.*

*(23) Regem Belial aliqui dicunt statim post Luciferum fuisse creatum, ideoque sentiunt ipsum esse patrem & seductorem*

*eorum qui ex Ordine ceciderunt. Cecidit enim prius inter alios digniores & sapientiores, qui præcedebant Michaëlem & alios cœlestes angelos, qui decrant. Quamvis autem Belial ipsos qui in terram dejecti fuerint, præcesserit: alios tamen qui in cœlo mansere, non antecessit. Cogitur hic divina virtute, cum accipit sacrificia, munera & holocausta, ut vicissim det immolantibus responsa vera: At per horam in veritate non perdurat, nisi potentia divina compellatur, ut dictum est. Angelicam assumit imagine in impense pulchram, in igneo curru sedens. Blande loquitur. Tribuit dignitates & prælaturas senatorias, gratiam item amicorum, & optimos famulos. Imperium habet octoginta legionum, ex ordine partim Virtutum, partim Angelorum. Forma exorcistæ invenitur in Vinculo Spirituum. Observandum exorcistæ, hunc Belial in omnibus succurrere suis subditis: Si autem se submittere noluerit, Vinculum Spirituum legatur, quo sapientissimus Salomon eos cum suis legionibus in vase vitreo relegavit: Et relegati cum omnibus legionibus fuere septuagintaduo reges, quorum primus erat Bileth, secundus Belial, deinde Asmoday, & circirer mille millia legionum. Illud proculdubio à magistro Salomone didiciste me fateor: Sed causam relegationis me non docuit, crediderim tamen propter arrogantiam ipsius Belial. Sunt quidam necromantici, qui asserunt, ipsum Salomonem quodam die astutia cujusdam mulieris seductum, orando se inclinasse versus simulacrum Belial nomine. Quod tamen fidem non meretur: Sed potius sentiendum, ut dictum est, propter superbiam & arrogantiam, relegatos esse in magno vase, projectos in Babylone in puteum grandem valde. Enimvero prudentissimus Salomon divina potentia suas exequebatur operationes, quæ etiam nunquam eum destituit: propterea simulachrum non adorasse ipsum sentiendum est, alioqui divina virtute spiritus cogere nequivisset. Hic autem Belial cum tribus regibus in puteo fuit. At Babylonienses ad hæc exhorrescentes, rati se thesaurum amplum in puteo inventuros, unanimi consilio in puteum descenderunt, detegeruntque & confregere vas, unde mox egressi captivi, in proprium locum porto sunt rejecti. Belial vero ingressus quoddam simulachrum, dabat responsa sibi immolantibus & sacrificantibus, ut testatur Tocz in dictis suis: Et Babylonienses adorantes sacrificaverunt eidem.*

*(24) Bune Dux magnus & fortis, apparet ut draco, tribus capitibus, tertium vero assimilatur homini. Muta loquitur voce: Mortuos locum mutare facit, & dæmones supra defunctorum sepulchra congregari: omnimodo hominem locupletat, redditque loquacem & sapientem: ad quæsita vere respondet. Huic legiones parent triginta.*

*(25) Forneus magnus Marchio, similis monstro marino, reddit hominem in Rhetoricis admirabilem, optima fama & linguarum peritia ornat, tam amicis quam inimicis gratum facit. Subsunt huic vigintinovem legiones, ex ordine partim Thronorum, partim Angelorum.*

*(26) Roneve Marchio & Comes, assimilatur monstro. Singularem in Rhetoricis intelligcntiam confert, famulos item fidos, linguarum cognitionem, amicorum & inimicorum favorem. Huic obediunt legiones novendecim.*

*(27) Berith Dux magnus & terribilis: tribus nuncupatur nominibus, à quibusdam Beal, à Judæis Berith, à necromanticis Bolfri. Prodit ut miles ruber cum vestitu rubro, & equo ejusdem coloris coronaque ornatus. Vere de præsentibus, præteritis & futuris respondet. Virtute divina per annulum magicæ artis ad horam scilicet cogitur. Mendax etiam est. In aurum cuncta metallorum genera mutat. Dignitatibus ornat easdemque confirmat: Claram subtilemque edit vocem. Viginti sex legiones huic subsunt.*

*(28) Astaroth Dux magnus & fortis, prodiens angelica specie turpissima, insidensque in dracone infernali, & viperam portans manu dextra. Vere respondet de præteritis, præsentibus, futuris & occultis. Libenter de spirituum*

*creatore, & eorundem lapsu loquitur, quomodo peccaverint & ceciderint. Se spontè non prolapsum esse dicit. Reddit hominem mire eruditum in artibus liberalibus. Quadraginta legionibus imperat. Ab hoc quilibet exocista caveat, ne prope nimis cum admittat, ob fœtorem intolerabilem quem expirat. Itaque annulum argenteum magicum in manu sua juxta faciem teneat, quo se ab injuria facile tuebitur.*

*(29) Forras vel Forcas magnus Præses est: visitur forma viri fortissimi, & in humana specie vires herbarum & lapidum preciosorum intelligit. Plene docet Logica, Ethica & corundem partes. Reddit hominem invisibilem, ingeniosum, loquacem & vivacem: Amissa recuperat, thesauros detegit. Dominium viginti novem legionum habet.*

*(30) Furfur Comes est magnus, apparens ut cervus cauda flammea. In omnibus mentitur, nisi in triangulum intro ducatur. Jussus angelicam assumit imaginem. Rauca loquitur voce: amorem inter virum & mulierem libenter conciliat: novit & concitare fulgura, coruscationes & tonitrua in iis partibus ubi jussum fuerit. De occultis & divinis rebus bene respondet. Imperat legionibus vigintisex.*

*(31) Marchocias magnus Marchio est. Se ostentat specie lupæ ferocissimæ cum alis gryphi, cauda serpentina, & ex ore nescio quid evomens. Quum hominis imaginem induit, pugnator est optimus. Ad quæsita vere respondet: fidelis in cunctis exorcistæ mandatis. Fuit ordinis Dominationum. Huic subjacent legiones triginta. Sperat se post mille ducentos annos ad septimum Thronum reversurum: sed ea spe falsus est.*

*(32) Malphas magnus Præses, conspicitur corvo similis: sed hominis idolum indutus rauca fatur voce. Domos & turres ingentes mire extruit, & obvios cito facit artifices maximos: Hostium vero ædes & turres dejicit. Famulos suppeditat non*

malos. Sacrificia libenter suscipit, at sacrificatores omnes fallit. Quadraginta huic parent legiones.

(33) Vepar, alias Separ, Dux magnus & fortis: Similis syreni: Ductor est aquarum & navium armis onustarum. Ut mare jussu magistri turgidum navibusque plenum appareat, efficit: contra inimicos exorcistæ per dies tres vulneribus putrescentibus vermesque producentibus homines inficit, à quibus tamen negotio absoluto sanantur omnes. Imperat legionibus vigintinovem.

(34) Sabnac, alias Salmac, Marchio magnus & fortis: prodit ut miles armatus, capite leonis, in pallido equo infidens. Hominis formam transmutat mire: Turres magnas armis plenas ædificat, item castra & civitates. Triginta dies ex mandato exorcistæ homini vulnera putrida & verminantia infligit. Familiares conciliat bonos: dominium exercens quinquaginta legionum.

(35) Sydonay, alias Asmoday, Rex magnus, fortis & potens: Visitur tribus capitibus, quorum primum assimilatur capiti tauri, alterum hominis, tertium arietis. Cauda ejus serpentina, ex ore flammam eructat, pedes anserini. Super dracone infernali sedet, in manu lanceam & vexillum portans. Præcedit alios qui sub potestate Amaymonis sunt. Cum hujus officia exercet exorcista, fit fortis, cautus & in pedibus stans: si vero coopertus fuerit, ut in omnibus detegatur, efficiet: Quod si non fecerit exorcista, ab Amaymone in cunctis decipietur: Sed mox cum ipsum in prædicta forma conspicit, appellabit illum nomine suo, inquiens: Tu vero es Asmoday. Ipse non negabit: Et mox ad terram. Dat annulum virtutum: Docet absolute Geometriam, Arithmeticam, Astronomiam, Mechanicam: Ad interrogata plene & vere respondet: Hominem reddit invisibilem: Loca thesaurorum ostendit & custodit, si fuerit de legionibus Amaymonis. In sua potestate legiones septuaginta duas habet.

*(36) Gaap, alias Tap, Præses magnus & Princeps: in signo Meridiei apparet: sed quum humanam assumit faciem Clm 849, fol 66r: Apparet in signo medici cum suscipit figuram humanam; est doctor opti m us mulierum, et facit ardere in amorem virorum , ductor est præcipuorum quatuor regum, tam potens ut Byleth. Extiterunt autem quidam necromantici, qui huic libamina & holocausta obtulere, & ut eundem evocarent, artem exercuere, dicentes sapientissimum Salomonem eam composuisse, quod falsum est: imo fuit Cham filius Noë, qui primus post diluvium cœpit malignos invocare spiritus, invocavit autem Byleth, & composuit artem in suo nomine, & librum, qui multis mathematicis est cognitus. Fiebant autem holocausta, libamina, munera, & multa nefaria, quæ operabantur exorcistæ admistis sanctissimis Dei nominibus, quæ in eadem arte sparsim exprimuntur. Epistola vero de iis nominibus est conscripta à Salomone, uti & scribunt Helias Hierosolymitanus & Heliseus. Notandum, si aliquis exorcista habuerit artem Beleth, nec ipsum coram se sistere possit aut videre, nisi per artem: Quomodo autem eundem continere oporteat, non est explicandum, quum sit nefandum, & nihil à Salomone de ejus dignitate & officio didicerim, hoc tamen non silebo, ipsum reddere hominem admirabilem in philosophia & artibus omnibus liberalibus. Facit ad amorem, odium, invisibilitatem & consecrationem eorum quæ sunt de dominatione Amaymonis: Et de potestate alterius exorcistæ tradit familiares, & vera perfecte responsa de præsentibus, præteritis & futuris. Velocissimo transcursu in varias regiones traducit hominem. Sexagintasex præest legionibus, & fuit de Potestatum ordine.*

*(37) Chax, alias Scox, Dux est & Marchio magnus: Similis ciconiæ rauca voce & subtili. Mirabiliter aufert visum, auditum & intellectum jussu exorcistæ: aufert pecuniam ex qualibet domo regia, & reportat post mille ducentos annos, si jussus fuerit: abripit & equos. Fidelis esse in omnibus mandatis putatur: ac licet se obsecuturum exorcistæ*

*promittat, non tamen in omnibus facit. Mendax est, nisi in triangulum introducatur: introductus autem loquitur de rebus divinis & reconditis thesauris, qui à malignis spiritibus non custodiuntur. Promittit insuper se collaturum optimos famulos, qui accepti sunt, si non fuerint deceptores. Huic subjacent legiones triginta.*

*(38) Pucel Dux magnus & fortis, apparet in specie angelica, sed obscura valde: loquitur de occultis: docet Geometriam & omnes artes liberales: sonitus facit ingentes, & sonare aquas ubi non sunt, easdem & calefacit & harum balnea recuperandæ sanitati servientia certis temporibus, distemperat jussu exorcistæ. Fuit de ordine Potestatum, habetque in sua potestate legiones quadragintaocto.*

*(39) Furcas miles est: prodit similitudine sævi hominis cum longa barba, & capillitio cano. In equo pallido insidet, portans in manu telum acutum. Docet perfecte practicam, philosophiam, rhetoricam, logicam, chiromantiam, astronomiam, piromantiam, & earum partes. Huic parent viginti legiones.*

*(40) Murmur magnus Dux & Comes: Apparet militis forma, equitans in vulture, & ducali corona comptus. Hunc præcedunt duo ministri tubis magnis: Philosophiam absolute docet. Cogit animas coram exorcista apparere, ut interrogatæ respondeant ad ipsius quæsita. Fuit de ordine partim Thronorum, partim Angelorum.*

*(41) Caym magnus Præses, formam assumens merulæ: at quum hominem induit, respondet in favilla ardente, ferens in manu glagium sic gladium acutissimum. Præ cæteris sapienter argumentari facit: Tribuit intellectum omnium volatilium, mugitus boum, latratus canum, & sonitus aquarum: de futuris optime respondet. Fuit ex ordine Angelorum. Præsidet legionibus triginta.*

*(42) Raum vel Raym Comes est magnus: Ut corvus visitur: Sed cum assumit humanam faciem, si ab exorcista jussus fuerit, mirè ex regis domo vel alia suffuratur, & ad locum sibi designatum transfert. Civitates destruit: Dignitatum despectum ingerit. Novit præsentia, præterita & futura. Favorem tam hostium quam amicorum conciliat. Fuit ex ordine Thronorum. Præest legionibus triginta.*

*(43) Halphas Comes magnus, prodit similis ciconiæ rauca voce. Insigniter ædificat oppida ampla armis plena: Bellum movet, & jussus, homines bellicosos ad designatum locum mittit obviam. Subsunt huic viginti sex legiones.*

*(44) Focalor Dux magnus, prodit velut homo, habens alas gryphi forma. Accepta humana figura, interficit homines & in aquis submergit. Imperat mari & vento, navesque bellicas subvertit. Notandum omni exorcistæ, si huic mandetur, ne homines lædat, libenter obsequitur. Sperat se post mille annos reversurum ad septimum Thronum, sed fallitur. Triginta legionibus imperat.*

*(45) Vine magnus Rex & Comes: se ostentat ut leo in equo nigro insidens, portansque viperam in manu. Amplas turres libenter ædificat: Lapideas domus extruit, rivos reddit turgidos: Ad exorcistæ mandatum respondet de occultis, maleficis, præsentibus, præteritis & futuris.*

*(46) Bifrons, monstri similitudine conspicitur. Ubi humanam assumit imaginem, reddit hominem in Astrologia mirabilem, planetarum mansiones absolute docens, idem præstat in Geometria, & mensuris aliis. Vires herbarum, lapidum pretiosorum & lignorum intelligit. Corpora mortuorum de loco ad locum transmutat: Candelas super defunctorum sepulchra inflammare videtur. Huic subjacent vinginti sex legiones.*

*(47) Gamygyn magnus Marchio:* in forma equi parvi visitur: at ubi hominis simulachrum assumit, raucam edit vocem, de omnibus artibus liberalibus differens: efficit quoque, ut coram exorcista conveniant animæ in mari exeuntes, & quæ degunt in purgatorio (quod dicitur Cartagra, id est, afflictio animarum) & corpora aërea suscipiunt, apparentque evidenter, & ad interrogata respondent. Permanet apud exorcistam, donec ipsius votum expleverit. Triginta legiones in sua habet potestate.

*(48) Zagam magnus Rex & Præses:* ut taurus prodit cum alis ad modum gryphi: sed assumpta hominis forma, reddit hominem ingeniosum: transmutat cuncta metallorum genera in monetas illius ditionis, & aquam in vinum, & è diverso: sanguinem quoque in oleum, & contra: & stultum in sapientem. Præest triginta tribus legionibus.

*(49) Orias Marchio magnus,* visitur ut leo, in equo fortissimo equitans, cauda serpentina: in dextera portat duos grandes serpentes etiam exibilantes. Callet planetarum mansiones, & vires sidereas perfecte docet. Transmutat homines: confert dignitates, prælaturas & confirmationes: Item amicorum & hostium favorem. Præsidet legionibus triginta.

*(50) Volac magnus Præses:* progreditur uti puer alis angeli, super dracone equitans duobus capitibus. De occultis thesauris perfecte respondet, & ubi serpentes videantur, quos & viribus dedestitutos tradit in exorcistæ manus. Dominium habet legionum triginta.

*(51) Gomory Dux fortis & potens:* apparet ut mulier pulcherrima: ac ducali cingitur corona, in camelo equitans. Bene & vere respondet de præteritis, præsentibus, futuris, & occultis thesauris ubi lateant. Conciliat amorem mulierum, & maxime puellarum. Imperat legionibus vigintisex.

*(52) Decarabia vel Carabia, magnus Rex & Comes: venit similis \*. Vires herbarum & lapidum pretiosorum novit: efficit ut aves coram exorcista volent, & velut familiares ac domesticæ morentur, bibant & cantillent suo more. Parent huic triginta legiones.*

*(53) Amduscias Dux magnus & fortis: procedit ut unicornu: in humana similiter forma, quando coram magistro suo se fistit: Et si præcipiatur, efficit facile ut tubæ & symphoniæ omniaque musicorum instrumentorum genera audiantur, nec tamen conspectui appareant: ut item arbores ad exorcistæ genu se inclinent. Optimus est una cum famulis. Imperium habet vigintinovem legionum.*

*(54) Andras magnus Marchio: visitur forma angelica, capite nycticoraci nigro simili, in lupo nigro & fortissimo equitans, bajulansque manu gladium acutissimum. Novit interficere dominum, servum & coadjutores: author est discordiarum. Dominatur legionibus triginta.*

*(55) Androalphus Marchio magnus, apparens ut pavo: graves edit sonitus: Et in humana forma docet perfecte geometriam & mensuram spectantia: reddit hominem in argumentando argutum, & in astronomia prudentem, eundemque in avis speciem transmutat. Triginta huic subsunt legiones.*

*(56) Oze Præses magnus, procedit similis leopardo: sed hominem mentitus, reddit prudentem in artibus liberalibus: vere resondet de divinis & occultis: transmutat hominis formam: & ad eam insaniam eum redigit, ut sibi persuadeat esse quod non est, quemadmodum se esse regem vel papam, & coronam in capite gestare: duratque id regnum horam.*

*(57) Aym vel Haborym Dux magnus & fortis: progreditur tribus capitibus, primo serpenti, simili, altero homini duos \* habenti, tertio felino. In vipera equitat, ingentem facem ardentem portans, cujus flamma succenditur castrum vel*

civitas. Omnibus modis ingeniosum reddit hominem: de abstrusis rebus vere respondet. Imperat legionibus vigintisex.

(58) Orobas magnus Princeps: procedit equo conformis: hominis autem indutus idoltum, de virtute divina loquitur: vera dat responsa de præteritis, præsentibus, futuris, de divinitate & creatione: neminem decipit, nec tentari sinit: confert prælaturas & dignitates, amicorum item & hostium favorem. Præsidet legionibus viginti.

(59) Vapula Dux magnus & fortis: conspicitur ut leo alis ad modum gryphi. Reddit hominem subtilem & mirabilem in artibus mechanicis, philosophia, & scientiis quæ in libris continentur. Præfectus est trigintasex legionum.

(60) Cimeries magnus Marchio & fortis: imperans in partibus Africanis: docet perfecte Grammaticam, Logicam & Rhetoricam. Thesauros detegit, & occulta aperit. Facit ut homo cursu celerrimo videatur transmutari in militem. Equitat in equo nigro & grandi. Legionibus viginti præest.

(61) Amy Præses magnus: apparet in flamma ignea: sed humana assumpta forma, reddit hominem admirabilem in astrologia & omnibus artibus liberalibus. Famulos suppetit optimos: thesauros à spiritibus custoditos ostendit. Præfecturam habet legionem triginta sex, ex ordine partim angelorum, partim potestatum. Sperat se post mille ducentos annos ad Thronum septimum reversurum, quod credibile non est.

(62) Flauros dux fortis: conspicitur forma leopardi & terribili. In humana specie vultum ostentat horrendum, & oculos flammeos. De præteritis, præsentibus & futuris plene & vere respondet. Si fuerit in triangulo, mentitut in cunctis, & fallit in aliis negotiis. Libenter loquitur de divinitate, mundi creatione & lapsu. Divina virtute cogitur, & omnes alii dæmones sive spiritus, ut omnes adversarios exorcistæ

*succendant & destruant. Et si virtute numinis ipsi imperatum fuerit, exorcistæ tentationem non permittit. Legiones viginti sub sua habet potestate.*

*(63) Balam Rex magnus & terribilis: prodit tribus capitibus, primo tauri, altero hominis, tertio arietis: cauda adhæc serpentina, oculis flammeis, equitans in urso fortissimo, & accipitrem in manu portans. Raucam edit vocem: perfectè responet de præteritis, præsentibus & futuris: reddit hominem & invisibilem & prudentem. Quadraginta legionibus præsidet, & fuit ex ordine dominationum.*

*(64) Alocer Dux magnus & fortis: procedit ut miles in equo vasto insidens: facies ejus leonina, rubicunda valde cum oculis flammeis: graviter loquitur: hominem reddit admirabilem in astronomia & in omnibus artibus liberalibus: confert bonam familiam; Dominatur triginta sex legionibus.*

*(65) Zaleos magnus Comes: apparet ut miles pulcherrimus in crocodilo equitans, & ducali ornatus corona, pacificus, &c.*

*(66) Wal Dux magnus & fortis: conspicitur ut dromedarius magnus ac terribilis: at in humana forma linguam sonat Ægyptiacam graviter. Hic præ cæteris amorem maxime mulierum conciliat: inde novit præsentia, præterita & futura: confert & gratiam amicorum atque inimicorum. De ordine fuit potestatum. Trigintaseptem legiones gubernat.*

*(67) Haagenti magnus Præses: ut taurus videtur, habens alas gryphi: sed assumpta facie humana, reddit hominem ingeniosum in quibuslibet: cuncta metalla in aurum transmutat, aquam in vinum, & ediverso. Tot legionibus imperat, quot Zagan.*

*(68) Phœnix magnus Marchio: apparet uti avis phœnix puerili voce: sed antequam se sistit coram exorcista, cantus emittit dulcissimos: tunc autem cavendum exorcistæ cum*

*suis sociis, ne suavitati cantus aures accommodent, sed ille mox huic jubeat humanam assumere speciem, tunc mire loquetur de cunctis scientiis admirandis. Poëta est optimus & obediens. Sperat se post mille ducentos annos ad septimum thronum rediturum. Viginti præest legionibus.*

*(69) Stolas magnus Princeps: prodit forma nycticoracis: coram exorcista hominis simulachrum suscipit, docetque absolutè astronomiam. Herbarum & lapidum pretiosorum vires intelligit. Vigintisex legiones huic subjacent.*

*Legio 6666.*


*Secretum secretorum tu operans sis secretus horum.*

*Observa horas in quibus quatuor reges, scilicet Amoymon rex Orientalis, Gorson rex Meridionalis, Zymymar rex Septentrionalis, Goap rex & princeps Occidentalis possunt constringi, à tertia hora usque ad meridiem, à nona hora usque ad vesperas.*

*Item Marchiones à nona usque ad completorium, vel à completorio usque ad finem diei.*

*Item Duces à prima usque ad meridiem: & observatur cœlum clarum.*

*Item Prælati in aliqua hora diei.*

*Item Milites ab aurora usque ad ortum solis, vel à vesperis usque ad finem solis.*

*Item Præses in aliqua hora diei non potest constringi, nisi rex cui paret, invocaretur, & nec in crepusculo noctis.*

*Item Comites omni hora diei, dum sunt in locis campestribus vel sylvestribus, quo homines non solent accedere, &c.*

Citatio Prædictorum spirituum.

*Ubi quem volueris spiritum, hujus nomen & officium supra cognosces: inprimis autem ab omni pollutione, minimum tres vel quatuor dies mundus esto in prima citatione, sic & spiritus postea obsequentiores erunt: fac & circulum, & voca spiritum cum multa intentione: primum vero annulum in manu contineto: inde hanc recitato benedictionem tuo nomine & socii, si præsto fuerit, & effectum tui instituti sortieris, nec detrimentum à spiritibus senties: imo tuæ animæ perditionem.*

2. In nomine Domini nostri Jesu Christi ✠ patris & ✠ filii & ✠ spiritus sancti: sancta trinitas & inseparabilis unitas te invoco, ut sis mihi salus & defensio & protectio corporis & animæ meæ, & omnium rerum mearum. Per virtutem sanctæ crucis ✠ & per virtutem passionis tuæ deprecor te domine Jesu Christe, per merita beatissimæ Mariæ virginis & matris tuæ atque omnium sanctorum tuorum, ut mihi concedas gratiam & potestatem divinam super omnes malignos spiritus, ut quoscunque nominibus invocavero, statim ex omni parte conveniant, & voluntatem meam perfecte adimpleant, quod mihi nihil nocentes, neque timorem inferentes, sed potius obedientes & ministrantes, tua districte virtute præcipiente, mandata mea perficiant, Amen. Sanctus sanctus sanctus dominus Deus Sabaoth, qui venturus es judicare vivos & mortuos: tu qui es & primus & novissimus, Rex regum & dominus dominantium Joth Aglanabrath El abiel anathi Enathiel Amazin sedomel gayes tolima Elias ischiros athanatos ymas heli Messias, per hæc tua sancta nomina & per omnia alia invoco te & obsecro te domine Jesu Christe, per tuam nativitatem, per baptismum tuum, per passionem & crucem tuam, per ascensionem tuam, per adventum spiritus sancti paracliti, per amaritudinem animæ

*tuæ; quando exivit de corpore tuo, per quinque vulnera tua, per sanguinem & aquam, quæ exierant de corpore tuo, per virtutem tuam, per sacramentum quod dedisti discipulis tuis pridie quam passus fuisti: per sanctam trinitatem, per individuam vnitatem, per beatam Mariam matrem tuam, per angelos & archangelos, per prophetas & patriarchas, & per omnes sanctos tuos, & per omnia sacramenta quæ fiunt in honore tuo: adoro te & obsecro te, benedico tibi & rogo, ut acceptes orationes has & conjurationes & verba oris mei, quibus uti voluero. Peto Domine Iesu Christe: da mihi virtutem & potestatem tuam super omnes angelos tuos, qui de cœlo ejecti sunt ad decipiendum genus humanum, ad attrahendum eos, ad constringendum, ad ligandum eos pariter & solvendum: Et ad congregandum eos coram me, & ad præcipiendum eis ut omnia, quæ possunt, faciant, & verba mea vocemque meam nullo modo contemnant: sed mihi & dictis meis obediant, & me timeant, per humanitatem & misericordiam & gratiam tuam deprecor & peto te adonay amay hortan vigedora mytay hel suranat ysion ysyesy & per omnia nomina tua sancta, per omnes sanctos & sanctas tuas per angelos & archangelos, potestates, dominationes & virtutes, & per illud nomen per quod Salomon contringebat dæmones, & conclusit ipsos Elhroch eban her agle goth joth othie venoch nabrat, & per omnia sacra nomina quæ scripta sunt in hoc libro & per virtutem eorundem, quatenus me potentem facias congregare & constringere omnes tuos spiritus de cœlo depulsos, ut mihi veraciter de omnibus meis interrogatis, de quibus quæram, responsionem veracem tribuant, & omnibus meis mandatis illi satisfaciant sine læsione corporis & animæ meæ & omnium ad me pertinentium, per Dominum nostrum Jesum Christum filium tuum, qui tecum vivit & regnat in unitate spiritus sancti Deus per omnia secula.*

*3. O pater omnipotens, ô fili sapiens, ô spiritus sancte corda hominum illustrans, ô vos tres in personis, una vero deitas in substantia: qui Adam & Evæ in peccatis eorum pepercistis, &*

*propter eorum peccata mortem subiisti tu fili turpissimam, in lignoque sanctæ crucis sustinuisti: ô misericordissime, quando ad tuam confugio misericordiam, & supplico modis omnibus quibus possum, per hæc nomina sancta tui filii, scilicet & , & per omnia alia sua nomina, quatenus concedas mihi virtutem & potestatem tuam, ut valeam tuos spiritus qui de cœlo ejecti sunt, ante me citare, & ut ipsi mecum loquantur, & mandata mea perficiant statim & sine mora, cum eorum voluntate, sine omni læsione corporis, animæ & bonorum meorum, &c. Continua ut in libro \* Annuli Salomonis continetur.*

*4. O summa & æterna virtus Altissimi, qui te disponente his judicio vocatis \* vaycheon stimulamaton ezphares tetragrammaton olyoram irion esytion existion eryona onela brasym noym messias sother emanuël sabaoth adonay, te adoro, te invoco, totius mentis viribus meis imploro, quatenus per te præsentes orationes & consecrationes & conjurationes consecrentur videlicet, & ubicunque maligni spiritus in virtute tuorum nominum sunt vocati, & omni parte conveniant, & voluntatem mei exorcisatoris diligenter adimpleant, fiat fiat fiat, Amen.*

*5. Hæc blasphema & execranda hujus mundi fæx & sentina pœnam in magos prophanos bene constitutam, pro scelerato mentis ausu jure meretur.*

*FINIS*

# PSEUDOMONARCHIA

# DÆMONUM

**Johann Weyer**

Translation in Reginald Scot
The Discoverie of Witchcraft

(1584)

*Johann Wier, Pseudomonarchia daemonum. Salomons notes of conjuration*

"Ah, human cares! Ah, how much futility in the world!"

-- C. Lucilius, Satires of Persius

An inventarie of the names, shapes, powers, governement, and effects of divels and spirits, of their severall segniories and degrees: a strange discourse woorth the reading.

# READER

(1) Baell. Their first and principall king (which is of the power of the east) is called Baëll who when he is conjured up, appeareth with three heads; the first, like a tode; the second, like a man; the third, like a cat. He speaketh with a hoarse voice, he maketh a man go invisible and wise, he hath under his obedience and rule sixtie and six legions of divels.

(2) Agares. The first duke under the power of the east, is named Agares, he commeth up mildile i.e. he appears willingly in the likenes of a faire old man, riding upon a crocodile, and carrieng a hawke on his fist; hee teacheth presentlie all maner of toongs, he fetcheth backe all such as runne awaie, and maketh them runne that stand still; he overthroweth all dignities supernaturall and temporall, hee maketh earthquakes, lit. "and makes spirits of the earth dance" and is of the order of vertues, having under his regiment thirtie one legions.

(3) Marbas, alias Barbas is a great president, and appeareth in the forme of a mightie lion; but at the commandement of a conjuror commeth up in the likenes of a man, and answereth fullie as touching anie thing which is hidden or secret: he bringeth diseases, and cureth them, he promoteth

wisedome, and the knowledge of mechanicall arts, or handicrafts; he changeth men into other shapes, and under his presidencie or gouvernement are thirtie six legions of divels conteined.

(4) Pruflas, otherwise found as Bufas, is a great prince and duke, whose abode is around the Tower of Babylon, and there he is seen like a flame outside. His head however is like that of a great night hawk. He is the author and promoter of discord, war, quarrels, and falsehood. He may not be admitted into every place. He responds generously to your requests. Under him are twenty-six legions, partly of the order of Thrones, and partly of the order of Angels.

(5) Amon, or Aamon, is a great and mightie marques, and commeth abroad in the likenes of a woolfe, having a serpents taile, spetting out and breathing vomiting flames of fier; when he putteth on the shape of a man, he sheweth out dogs teeth, and a great head like to a mightie raven night hawk ; he is the strongest prince of all other, and understandeth of all things past and to come, he procureth favor, and reconcileth both freends and foes, and ruleth fourtie legions of divels.

(6) Barbatos, a great countie or earle, and also a duke, he appeareth in Signo sagittarii sylvestris, with foure kings, which bring companies and great troopes. He understandeth the singing of birds, the barking of dogs, the lowings of bullocks, and the voice of all living creatures. He detecteth treasures hidden by magicians and inchanters, and is of the order of vertues, which in part beare rule: he knoweth all things past, and to come, and reconcileth freends and powers; and governeth thirtie legions of divels by his authoritie.

(7) Buer is a great president, and is seene in this signe * ; he absolutelie teacheth philosophie morall and naturall, and

also logicke, and the vertue of herbes: he giveth the best familiars, he can heale all diseases, speciallie of men, and reigneth over fiftie legions.

(8) Gusoin Gusoyn is a great duke, and a strong, appearing in the forme of a Xenophilus, he answereth all things, present, past, and to come, expounding all questions. He reconcileth freendship, and distributeth honours and dignities, and ruleth over fourtie and five legions of divels.

(9) Botis, otherwise Otis, a great president and an earle he commeth foorth in the shape of an ouglie lit. 'worst' viper, and if he put on humane shape, he sheweth great teeth, and two hornes, carrieng a sharpe sword in his hand: he giveth answers of things present, past, and to come, and reconcileth friends, and foes, ruling sixtie legions.

(10) Bathin Bathym, sometimes called Mathim Marthim, a great duke and a strong, he is seene in the shape of a verie strong man, with a serpents taile, sitting on a pale horsse, understanding the vertues of hearbs and pretious stones, transferring men suddenlie from countrie to countrie, and ruleth thirtie legions of divels.

(11) Purson Pursan, alias Curson, a great king, he commeth foorth like a man with a lions face, carrieng a most cruell viper, and riding on a beare; and before him go alwaies trumpets, he knoweth things hidden, and can tell all things present, past, and to come: he discloses hidden things, he bewraieth treasure, he can take a bodie either humane or aierie; he answereth truelie of all things earthlie and secret, of the divinitie and creation of the world, and bringeth foorth the best familiars; and there obeie him two and twentie legions of divels, partlie of the order of vertues, & partlie of the order of thrones.

(12) Eligor, alias Abigor, is a great duke, and appeereth as a goodlie handsome knight, carrieng a lance, an ensigne, and a scepter: he answereth fullie of things hidden, and of warres, and how souldiers should meete: he knoweth things to come, and procureth the favour of lords and knights, governing sixtie legions of divels.

(13) Leraie Loray , alias Oray, a great marquesse, shewing himselfe in the likenesse of a galant handsome archer, carrieng a bowe and a quiver, he is author of all battels, he dooth putrifie all such wounds as are made with arrowes by archers, Quos optimos objicit tribus diebus, who best drives away mobs from the days (?) and he hath regiment over thirtie legions.

(14) Valefar, alias Malephar Malaphar , is a strong duke, comming foorth in the shape of a lion, and the head of a theefe or "barking" , he is verie familiar with them to whom he maketh himself acquainted, till he hath brought them to the gallowes, and ruleth ten legions.

(15) Morax, alias Foraii, a great earle and a president, he is seene like a bull, and if he take unto him a mans face, he maketh men wonderfull cunning in astronomie, & in all the liberall sciences: he giveth good familiars and wise, knowing the power & vertue of hearbs and stones which are pretious, and ruleth thirtie six legions.

(16) Ipos Ipes , alias Ayporos Ayperos , is a great earle and a prince, appeering in the shape of an angell, and yet indeed more obscure and filthie than a lion, with a lions head, a gooses feet, and a hares taile: he knoweth things to come and past, he maketh a man wittie, and bold, and hath under his jurisdiction thirtie six legions.

(17) Naberius Naberus , alias Cerberus, is a valiant marquesse, shewing himselfe in the forme of a crowe, when

he speaketh with a hoarse voice: he maketh a man amiable and cunning in all arts, and speciallie in rhetorike, he procureth the losse of prelacies and dignities: nineteene legions heare and obeie him.

(18) Glasya Labolas, alias Caacrinolaas, or Caassimolar, is a great president, who commeth foorth like a dog, and hath wings like a griffen, he giveth the knowledge of arts, and is the captaine of all mansleiers: he understandeth things present and to come, he gaineth the minds and love of freends and foes, he maketh a man go invisible, and hath the rule of six and thirtie legions.

(19) Zepar is a great duke, appearing as a souldier, inflaming women with the loove of men, and when he is bidden he changeth their shape, untill they maie enjoie their beloved, he also maketh them barren, and six and twentie legions are at his obeie and commandement.

(20) Bileth Byleth is a great king and a terrible, riding on a pale horsse, before whome go trumpets, and all kind of melodious musicke. When he is called up by an exorcist, he appeareth rough turgid and furious, to deceive him. Then let the exorcist or conjuror take heed to himself; and to allaje his courage, let him hold a hazell bat rod, staff, or stick in his hand, wherewithall he must reach out toward the east and south, and make a triangle without besides the circle; but if he hold not out his hand unto him, and he bid him come in, and he still refuse the bond or chain of spirits; let the conjuror proceed to reading, and by and by he will submit himselfe, and come in, and doo whatsoever the exorcist commandeth him, and he shalbe safe. If Bileth the king be more stubborne, and refuse to enter into the circle at the first call, and the conjuror shew himselfe fearfull, or if he have not the chaine of spirits, certeinelie he will never feare nor regard him after. Also, if the place be unapt for a triangle to be made without the circle, then set there a boll

of wine, and the exorcist shall certeinlie knowe when he commeth out of his house, with his fellowes, and that the foresaid Bileth will be his helper, his friend, and obedient unto him when he commeth foorth. And when he commeth, let the exorcist receive him courteouslie, and glorifie him in his pride, and therfore he shall adore him as other kings doo, bicause he saith nothing without other princes. Also, if he be cited by an exorcist, alwaies a silver ring of the middle finger of the left hand must be held against the exorcists face, as they doo for Amaimon. And the dominion and power of so great a prince is not to be pretermitted; for there is none under the power & dominion of the conjuror, but he that deteineth both men and women in doting better: "foolish" or "silly" love, till the exorcist hath had his pleasure. He is of the orders of powers, hoping to returne to the seaventh throne, which is not altogether credible, and he ruleth eightie five legions.

(21) Sitri Sytry , alias Bitru, is a great prince, appeering with the face of a leopard, and having wings as a griffen: when he taketh humane shape, he is verie beautiful, he inflameth a man with a womans love, and also stirreth up women to love men, being commanded he willinglie deteineth discloses secrets of women, laughing at them and mocking them, to make them luxuriouslie naked, and there obeie him sixtie legions.

(22) Paimon is more obedient in Lucifer than other kings are. Lucifer is heere to be understood he that was drowned in the depth of his knowledge: he would needs be like God, and for his arrogancie was throwne out into destruction, of whome it is said; Everie pretious stone is thy covering (Ezech. 88  28.13 .). Paimon is constrained by divine vertue to stand before the exorcist; where he putteth on the likenesse of a man: he sitteth on a beast called a dromedarie, which is a swift runner, and weareth a glorious crowne, and hath an effeminate countenance. There goeth before him an

host of men with trumpets and well sounding cymbals, and all musicall instruments. At the first he appeereth with a great crie and roring, as in Circulo Empto. Salomonis, and in the art is declared. And if this Paimon speake sometime that the conjuror understand him not, let him not therefore be dismaied. But when he hath delivered him the first obligation to observe his desire, he must bid him also answer him distinctlie and plainelie to the questions he shall aske you, of all philosophie, wisedome, and science, and of all other secret things. And if you will knowe the disposition of the world, and what the earth is, or what holdeth it up in the water, or any other thing, or what is Abyssus, or where the wind is, or from whence it commeth, he will teach you aboundantlie. Consecrations also as well of sacrifices offerings, libations as otherwise may be reckoned. He giveth dignities and confirmations; he bindeth them that resist him in his owne chaines, and subjecteth them to the conjuror; he prepareth good familiars, and hath the understanding of all arts. Note, that at the calling up of him, the exorcist must looke towards the northwest, bicause there is his house. When he is called up, let the exorcist receive him constantlie without feare, let him aske what questions or demands he list, and no doubt he shall obteine the same of him. And the exorcist must beware he forget not the creator, for those things, which have beene rehearsed before of Paimon, some saie he is of the order of dominations; others saie, of the order of cherubim. There follow him two hundred legions, partlie of the order of angels, and partlie of potestates. Note that if Paimon be cited alone by an offering or sacrifice, two kings followe him; to wit, Beball & Abalam, & other potentates: in his host are twentie five legions, bicause the spirits subject to them are not alwaies with them, except they be compelled to appeere by divine vertue.

(23) Some saie that the king Beliall was created immediatlie after Lucifer, and therefore they thinke that he was father

and seducer of them which fell being of the orders. For he fell first among the worthier and wiser sort, which went before Michael and other heavenlie angels, which were lacking. Although Beliall went before all them that were throwne downe to the earth, yet he went not before them that tarried in heaven. This Beliall is constrained by divine venue, when he taketh sacrifices, gifts, and burnt offerings, that he againe may give unto the offerers true answers. But he tarrieth not one houre in the truth, except he be constrained by the divine power, as is said. He taketh the forme of a beautifull angell, sitting in a firie chariot; he speaketh faire, he distributeth preferments of senatorship, and the favour of friends, and excellent familiars: he hath rule over eightie legions, partlie of the order of vertues, partlie of angels; he is found in the forme of an exorcist in the bonds of spirits. The exorcist must consider, that this Beliall doth in everie thing assist his subjects. If he will not submit himselfe, let the bond of spirits be read: the spirits chaine is sent for him, wherewith wise Salomon gathered them togither with their legions in a brasen vessell, where were inclosed among all the legions seventie two kings, of whome the cheefe was Bileth, the second was Beliall, the third Asmoday, and above a thousand thousand legions. Without doubt (I must confesse) I learned this of my maister Salomon; but he told me not why he gathered them together, and shut them up so: but I beleeve it was for the pride of this Beliall. Certeine nigromancers doo saie, that Salomon, being on a certeine daie seduced by the craft of a certeine woman, inclined himselfe to praie before the same idoll, Beliall by name: which is not credible. And therefore we must rather thinke (as it is said) that they were gathered together in that great brasen vessell for pride and arrogancie, and throwne into a deepe lake or hole in Babylon. For wise Salomon did accomplish his workes by the divine power, which never forsooke him. And therefore we must thinke he worshipped not the image Beliall; for then he could not have constrained the spirits by divine vertue: for this Beliall, with three kings were in the lake. But the Babylonians woondering at the matter, supposed that they should find therein a great quantitie of treasure, and therefore with one consent went downe into the lake, and uncovered and brake the vessell, out of the which immediatlie flew the capteine divels, and were delivered to their former and proper places. But this Beliall entred into a certeine image, and there gave answer to them that offered and sacrificed unto him: as Tocz. in his sentences reporteth, and the Babylonians did worship and sacrifice thereunto.

(24) Bune is a great and a strong Duke, he appeareth as a dragon with three heads, the third whereof is like to a man; he speaketh with a divine voice, he maketh the dead to change their place, and divels to assemble upon the sepulchers of the dead: he greatlie inricheth a man, and maketh him eloquent and wise, answering trulie to all demands, and thirtie legions obeie him.

(25) Forneus is a great marquesse, like unto a monster of the sea, he maketh men woondeffull in rhetorike, he adorneth a man with a good name, and the knowledge of toongs, and maketh one beloved as well of foes as freends: there are under him nine and twentie legions, of the order partlie of thrones, and partlie of angels.

(26) Ronove Roneve a marquesse and an earle, he is resembled to a monster, he bringeth singular understanding in rhetorike, faithfull servants, knowledge of toongs, favour of freends and foes; and nineteene legions obeie him.

(27) Berith is a great and a terrible duke, and hath three names. Of some he is called Beall; of the Jewes Berithi Berith; of Nigromancers Bolfry Bolfri: he commeth foorth as a red souldier, with red clothing, and upon a horsse of that colour, and a crowne on his head. He answereth trulie of things present, past, and to come. He is compelled at a

certeine houre, through divine vertue, by a ring of art magicke. He is also a lier, he turneth all mettals into gold, he adorneth a man with dignities, and confirmeth them, he speaketh with a cleare and a subtill voice, and six and twentie legions are under him.

(28) Astaroth is a great and a strong duke, comming foorth in the shape of a fowle angell, sitting upon an infernall dragon, and carrieng on his right hand a viper: he answereth trulie to matters present, past, and to come, and also of all secrets. He talketh willinglie of the creator of spirits, and of their fall, and how they sinned and fell: he saith he fell not of his owne accord. He maketh a man woonderfull learned in the liberall sciences, he ruleth fourtie legions. Let everie exorcist take heed, that he admit him not too neere him, bicause of his stinking breath lit. "because of the intolerable stench which he exhales" . And therefore let the conjuror hold neere to his face a magicall silver ring, and that shall defend him.

(29) Foras Forras , alias Forcas is a great president, and is seene in the forme of a strong man, and in humane shape, he understandeth the vertue of hearbs and pretious stones: he teacheth fullie logicke, ethicke, and their parts: he maketh a man invisible, wittie, eloquent, and to live long; he recovereth things lost, and discovereth discloses treasures, and is lord over nine and twentie legions.

(30) Furfur is a great earle, appearing as an hart, with a firie taile, he lieth in everie thing, except he be brought up within a triangle; being bidden, he taketh angelicall forme, he speaketh with a hoarse voice, and willinglie maketh love betweene man and wife or simply "woman"; he raiseth thunders and lightnings, and blasts. Where he is commanded, he answereth well, both of secret and also of divine things, and hath rule and dominion over six and twentie legions.

(31) Marchosias Marchocias is a great marquesse, he sheweth himselfe in the shape of a cruell shee woolfe, with a griphens wings, with a serpents taile, and spetting I cannot tell what out of his mouth. When he is in a mans shape, he is an excellent fighter, he answereth all questions trulie, he is faithfull in all the conjurors businesse commands, he was of the order of dominations, under him are thirtie legions: he hopeth after 1200. yeares to returne to the seventh throne, but he is deceived in that hope.

(32) Malphas is a great president, he is seene like a crowe, but being cloathed with humane image, speaketh with a hoarse voice, be buildeth houses and high towres wonderfullie, and quicklie bringeth artificers togither, he throweth downe also the enimies edifications, he helpeth to good familiars, he receiveth sacrifices willinglie, but he deceiveth all the sacrificers, there obeie him fourtie legions.

(33) Vepar, alias Separ, a great duke and a strong, he is like a mermaid, he is the guide of the waters, and of ships laden with armour; he bringeth to passe (at the commandement of his master) that the sea shalbe rough and stormie, and shall appeare full of shippes; he killeth men in three daies, with putrifieng their wounds, and producing maggots into them; howbeit, they maie be all healed with diligence, he ruleth nine and twentie legions.

(34) Sabnacke Sabnac, alias Salmac, is a great marquesse and a strong, he commeth foorth as an armed soldier with a lions head, sitting on a pale horsse, he dooth marvelouslie change mans forme and favor, he buildeth high towres full of weapons, and also castels and cities; he inflicteth men thirtie daies with wounds both rotten and full of maggots, at the exorcists commandement, he provideth good familiars, and hath dominion over fiftie legions.

(35) Sidonay Sydonay, alias Asmoday, a great king, strong and mightie, he is seene with three heads, whereof the first is like a bull, the second like a man, the third like a ram, he hath a serpents taile, he belcheth flames out of his mouth, he hath feete like a goose, he sitteth on an infernall dragon, he carrieth a lance and a flag in his hand, he goeth before others, which are under the power of Amaymon. When the conjuror exerciseth this office, let him be abroad brave, let him be warie courageous and standing on his feete; if his cap be on his head! if he is afraid he will be overwhelmed, he will cause all his dooings to be bewraied divulged, which if he doo not, the exorcist shalbe deceived by Amaymon in everie thing. But so soone as he seeth him in the forme aforesaid, he shall call him by his name, saieng; Thou art Asmoday; he will not denie it, and by and by he boweth downe to the ground; he giveth the ring of venues, he absolutelie teacheth geometrie, arythmetike, astronomie, and handicrafts mechanics. To all demands he answereth fullie and trulie, he maketh a man invisible, he sheweth the places where treasure lieth, and gardeth it, if it be among the legions of Amaymon, he hath under his power seventie two legions.

(36) Gaap, alias Tap, a great president and a prince, he appeareth in a meridionall signe, and when he taketh humane shape Clm 849 reads: He appears in the form of a doctor when he takes on a human form. He is the most excellent doctor of women, and he makes them burn with love for men. he is the guide of the foure principall kings, as mightie as Bileth. There were certeine necromancers that offered sacrifices and burnt offerings unto him; and to call him up, they exercised an art, saieng that Salomon the wise made it. Which is false: for it was rather Cham, the sonne of Noah, who after the floud began first to invocate wicked spirits. He invocated Bileth, and made an art in his name, and a booke which is knowne to manie mathematicians. There were burnt offerings and sacrifices made, and gifts

given, and much wickednes wrought by the exorcists, who mingled therewithall the holie names of God, the which in that art are everie where expressed. Marie Certainly there is an epistle of those names written by Salomon, as also write Helias Hierosolymitanus and Helisæus. It is to be noted, that if anie exorcist have the art of Bileth, and cannot make him stand before him, nor see him, I may not bewraie how and declare the meanes to conteine him, bicause it is abhomination, and for that I have learned nothing from Salomon of his dignitie and office. But yet I will not hide this; to wit, that he maketh a man woonderfull in philosophie and all the liberall sciences: he maketh love, hatred, insensibilitie, invisibilitie, consecration, and consecration of those things that are belonging unto the domination of Amaymon, and delivereth familiars out of the possession of other conjurors, answering truly and perfectly of things present, past, & to come, & transferreth men most speedilie into other nations, he ruleth sixtie six legions, & was of the order of potestats.

(37) Shax Chax, alias Scox, is a darke and a great marquesse, like unto a storke, with a hoarse and subtill voice: he dooth marvellouslie take awaie the sight, hearing and understanding of anie man, at the commandement of the conjuror: he taketh awaie monie out of everie kings house, and carrieth it backe after 1200. yeares, if he be commanded, he is a horssestealer, he is thought to be faithfull in all commandements: and although he promise to be obedient to the conjuror in all things; yet is he not so, he is a lier, except he be brought into a triangle, and there he speaketh divinelie, and telleth of things which are hidden, and not kept of wicked spirits, he promiseth good familiars, which are accepted if they be not deceivers, he hath thirtie legions.

(38) Procell is a great and a strong duke, appearing in the shape of an angell, but speaketh verie darklie of things

hidden, he teacheth geometrie and all the liberall arts, he maketh great noises, and causeth the waters to rore, where are none, he warmeth waters, and distempereth bathes at certeine times, as the exorcist appointeth him, he was of the order of potestats, and hath fourtie eight legions under his power.

(39) Furcas is a knight and commeth foorth in the similitude of a cruell man, with a long beard and a hoarie head, he sitteth on a pale horsse, carrieng in his hand a sharpe weapon dart or spear, he perfectlie teacheth practike philosophie, rhetorike, logike, astronomie, chiromancie, pyromancie, and their parts: there obeie him twentie legions.

(40) Murmur is a great duke and an earle, appearing in the shape of a souldier, riding on a griphen vulture, with a dukes crowne on his head; there go before him two of his ministers, with great trumpets, he teacheth philosophie absolutelie, he constraineth soules to come before the exorcist, to answer what he shall aske them, he was of the order partlie of thrones, and partlie of angels, and ruleth thirtie legions.

(41) Caim Caym is a great president, taking the forme of a thrush blackbird, but when he putteth on man's shape, he answereth in burning ashes, carrieng in his hand a most sharpe swoord, he maketh the best disputers, he giveth men the understanding of all birds, of the lowing of bullocks, and barking of dogs, and also of the sound and noise of waters, he answereth best of things to come, he was of the order of angels, and ruleth thirtie legions of divels.

(42) Raum, or Raim is a great earle, he is seene as a crowe, but when he putteth on humane shape, at the commandement of the exorcist, he stealeth woonderfullie out of the kings house, and carrieth it whether he is

assigned, he destroieth cities, and hath great despite unto dignities, he knoweth things present, past, and to come, and reconcileth freends and foes, he was of the order of thrones, and governeth thirtie legions.

(43) Halphas is a great earle, and commeth abroad like a storke, with a hoarse voice, he notablie buildeth up townes full of munition and weapons, he sendeth men of warre to places appointed, and hath under him six and twentie legions.

(44) Focalor is a great duke comming foorth as a man, with wings like a griphen, he killeth men, and drowneth them in the waters, and overturneth ships of warre, commanding and ruling both winds and seas. And let the conjuror note, that if he bid him hurt no man, he willinglie consenteth thereto: he hopeth after 1000. yeares to returne to the seventh throne, but he is deceived, he hath three legions.

(45) Vine is a great king and an earle, he showeth himselfe as a lion, riding on a blacke horsse, and carrieth a viper in his hand, he gladlie buildeth large towres, he throweth downe stone walles, and maketh waters rough. At the commandement of the exorcist he answereth of things hidden, of witches, and of things present, past, and to come.

(46) Bifrons is seene in the similitude of a monster, when he taketh the image of a man, he maketh one woonderfull cunning in astrologie, absolutelie declaring the mansions of the planets, he dooth the like in geometrie, and other admesurements, he perfectlie understandeth the strength and vertue of hearbs, pretious stones, and woods, he changeth dead bodies from place to place, he seemeth to light candles upon the sepulchres of the dead, and hath under him six and twentie legions.

(47) Gamigin  Gamygyn  is a great marquesse, and is seene in the forme of a little horsse, when he taketh humane shape he speaketh with a hoarse voice, disputing of all liberall sciences; he bringeth also to passe, that the soules, which are drowned in the sea, or which dwell in purgatorie (which is called Cartagra, that is, affliction of soules) shall take aierie bodies, and evidentlie appeare and answer to interrogatories at the conjurors commandement; he tarrieth with the exorcist, untill he have accomplished his desire, and hath thirtie legions under him.

(48) Zagan  Zagam  is a great king and a president, he commeth abroad like a bull, with griphens wings, but when he taketh humane shape, he maketh men wittie, he turneth all mettals into the coine of that dominion, and turneth water into wine, and wine into water, he also turneth bloud into wine oil, & wine oil into bloud, & a foole into a wise man, he is head of thirtie and three legions.

(49) Orias is a great marquesse, and is seene as a lion riding on a strong horsse, with a serpents taile, and carrieth in his right hand two great serpents hissing, he knoweth the mansion of planets and perfectlie teacheth the vertues of the starres, he transformeth men, he giveth dignities, prelacies, and confirmations, and also the favour of freends and foes, and hath under him thirtie legions.

(50) Valac  Volac  is a great president, and commeth abroad with angels wings like a boie, riding on a twoheaded dragon, he perfectlie answereth of treasure hidden, and where serpents may be seene, which he delivereth into the conjurors hands, void of anie force or strength, and hath dominion over thirtie legions of divels.

(51) Gomory a strong and a mightie duke, he appeareth like a faire woman, with a duchesse crownet about hir midle, riding on a camell, he answereth well and truelie of things

present, past, and to come, and of treasure hid, and where it lieth: he procureth the love of women, especiallie of maids, and hath six and twentie legions.

(52) Decarabia or Carabia, he commeth like a and knoweth the force of herbes and pretious stones, and maketh all birds flie before the exorcist, and to tarrie with him, as though they were tame, and that they shall drinke and sing, as their maner is, and hath thirtie legions.

(53) Amduscias a great and a strong duke, he commeth foorth as an unicorne, when he standeth before his maister in humane shape, being commanded, he easilie bringeth to passe, that trumpets and all musicall instruments may be heard and not seene, and also that trees shall bend and incline, according to the conjurors will, he is excellent among familiars, and hath nine and twentie legions.

(54) Andras is a great marquesse, and is seene in an angels shape with a head like a blacke night raven, riding upon a blacke and a verie strong woolfe, flourishing with a sharpe sword in his hand, he can kill the maister, the servant, and all assistants, he is author of discords, and ruleth thirtie legions.

(55) Andrealphus Androalphus is a great marquesse, appearing as a pecocke, he raiseth great noises, and in humane shape perfectlie teacheth geometrie, and all things belonging to admeasurements, he maketh a man to be a subtill disputer, and cunning in astronomie, and transformeth a man into the likenes of a bird, and there are under him thirtie legions.

(56) Ose Oze is a great president, and commeth foorth like a leopard, and counterfeting to be a man, he maketh one cunning in the liberall sciences, he answereth truelie of divine and secret things, he transformeth a mans shape, and

bringeth a man to that madnes or, "drives insanity away", that he thinketh himselfe to be that which he is not; as that he is a king or a pope, or that he weareth a crowne on his head, Durátque id regnum ad horam and makes the kingdom of time endure.

(57) Aym or Haborim Haborym is a great duke and a strong, he commeth foorth with three heads, the first like a serpent, the second like a man having two the third like a cat, he rideth on a viper, carrieng in his hand a light fier brand, with the flame whereof castels and cities are fiered, he maketh one wittie everie kind of waie, he answereth truelie of privie matters, and reigneth over twentie six legions.

(58) Orobas is a great prince, he commeth foorth like a horsse, but when he putteth on him a mans idol image, he talketh of divine vertue, he giveth true answers of things present, past, and to come, and of the divinitie, and of the creation, he deceiveth none, nor suffereth anie to be tempted, he giveth dignities and prelacies, and the favour of freends and foes, and hath rule over twentie legions.

(59) Vapula is a great duke and a strong, he is seene like a lion with griphens wings, he maketh a man subtill and wonderfull in handicrafts mechanics, philosophie, and in sciences conteined in bookes, and is ruler over thirtie six legions.

(60) Cimeries is a great marquesse and a strong, ruling in the parts of Aphrica Africa; he teacheth perfectlie grammar, logicke, and rhetorike, he discovereth treasures and things hidden, he bringeth to passe, that a man shall seeme with expedition to be turned into a soldier, he rideth upon a great blacke horsse, and ruleth twentie legions.

(61) Amy is a great president, and appeareth in a flame of fier, but having taken mans shape, he maketh one marvelous in astrologie, and in all the liberall sciences, he procureth excellent familiars, he bewraieth treasures preserved by spirits, he hath the governement of thirtie six legions, he is partlie of the order of angels, partlie of potestats, he hopeth after a thousand two hundreth yeares to returne to the seventh throne: which is not credible.

(62) Flauros a strong duke, is seene in the forme of a terrible strong leopard, in humane shape, he sheweth a terrible countenance, and fierie eies, he answereth trulie and fullie of things present, past, and to come; if he be in a triangle, he lieth in all things and deceiveth in other things, and beguileth in other busines, he gladlie talketh of the divinitie, and of the creation of the world, and of the fall; he is constrained by divine vertue, and so are all divels or spirits, to burne and destroie all the conjurors adversaries. And if he be commanded, he suffereth the conjuror not to be tempted, and he hath twentie legions under him.

(63) Balam is a great and a terrible king, he commeth foorth with three heads, the first of a bull, the second of a man, the third of a ram, he hath a serpents taile, and flaming eies, riding upon a furious very powerful beare, and carrieng a hawke on his fist, he speaketh with a hoarse voice, answering perfectlie of things present, past, and to come, hee maketh a man invisible and wise, hee governeth fourtie legions, and was of the order of dominations.

(64) Allocer Alocer is a strong duke and a great, he commeth foorth like a soldier, riding on a great horsse, he hath a lions face, verie red, and with flaming eies, he speaketh with a big voice, he maketh a man woonderfull in astronomie, and in all the liberall sciences, he bringeth good familiars, and ruleth thirtie six legions.

(65) Saleos Zaleos is a great earle, he appeareth as a gallant handsome soldier, riding on a crocodile, and weareth a dukes crowne, peaceable, &c.

(66) Vuall Wal is a great duke and a strong, he is seene as a great and terrible dromedarie, but in humane forme, he soundeth out in a base deep voice the Ægyptian toong. This man above all other procureth the especially love of women, and knoweth things present, past, and to come, procuring the love of freends and foes, he was of the order of potestats, and governeth thirtie seven legions.

(67) Haagenti is a great president, appearing like a great bull, having the wings of a griphen, but when he taketh humane shape, he maketh a man wise in everie thing, he changeth all mettals into gold, and changeth wine and water the one into the other, and commandeth as manie legions as Zagan.

(68) Phoenix is a great marquesse, appearing like the bird Phoenix, having a childs voice: but before he standeth still before the conjuror, he singeth manie sweet notes. Then the exorcist with his companions must beware he give no eare to the melodie, but must by and by bid him put on humane shape; then will he speake marvellouslie of all woonderfull sciences. He is an excellent poet, and obedient, he hopeth to returne to the seventh throne after a thousand two hundreth yeares, and governeth twentie legions.

(69) Stolas is a great prince, appearing in the forme of a nightraven, before the exorcist, he taketh the image and shape of a man, and teacheth astronomie, absolutelie understanding the vertues of herbes and pretious stones; there are under him twentie six legions.

Note that a legion is 6 6 6 6, and now by multiplication count how manie legions doo arise out of everie particular.

This was the work of one T. R. written in faire letters of red & blacke upõ parchment, and made by him, Ann. 1570. to the maintenance of his living, the edifieng of the poore, and the glorie of gods holie name: as he himselfe saith.

The secret of secrets; Thou that workst them, be secret in them.

# CHAPTER III

**THE HOURES WHERIN PRINCIPALL DIVELS MAY BE BOUND, TO WIT, RAISED AND RESTRAINED FROM DOOING OF HURT.**

AMAYMON king of the east, Gorson king of the south, Zimimar king of the north, Goap king and prince of the west, may be bound from the third hour, till noone, and from the ninth houre till evening.

Marquesses may be bound from the ninth houre till compline, and from compline till the end of the daie.

Dukes may be hound from the first houre till noone; and cleare wether is to be observed.

Prelates may be bound in anie houre of the daie.

Knights from daie dawning, till sunne rising; or from evensong, till the sunne set.

A President may not be bound in anie houre of the daie, except the king, whome he obeieth, be invocated; nor in the shutting of the evening.

Counties or erles may be bound at anie houre of the daie, so it be in the woods or feelds, where men resort not.

# CHAPTER IV

**THE FORME OF ADJURING OR CITING OF THE SPIRITS AFORESAID TO ARISE AND APPEARE**

WHEN you will have anie spirit, you must know his name and office; you must also fast, and be cleane from all pollution, three or foure daies before; so will the spirit be the more obedient unto you. Then make a circle, and call up the spirit with great intention, and holding a ring in your hand, rehearse in your owne name, and your companions (for one must alwaies be with you) this praier following, and so no spirit shall annoie you, and your purpose shall take effect. (And note how this agreeth with popish charmes and conjurations.)

In the name of our Lord Jesus Christ the ✚ father ✚ and the sonne ✚ and the Hollie-ghost ✚ holie trinitie and unseparable unitie, I call upon thee, that thou maiest be my salvation and defense, and the protection of my bodie and soule, and of all my goods through the vertue of thy holie crosse, and through the vertue of thy passion, I beseech thee O Lord Jesus Christ, by the merits of thy blessed mother S. Marie, and of all thy saints, that thou give me grace and divine power over all the wicked spirits, so as which of them soever I doo call by name, they may come by and by from everie coast, and accomplish my will, that they neither be hurtfull or fearefull unto me, but rather obedient and diligent about me. And through thy vertue streightlie commanding them, let them fulfill my commandements, Amen. Holie, holie, Lord God of sabboth, which wilt come to judge the quicke and the dead, thou which art A and Omega, first and last, King of kings and Lord of lords, Ioth, Aglanabrath, El, Abiel, Anathiel anathi Enathiel , Amazim, Sedomel, Gayes, Tolima, Elias, Ischiros, Athanatos, Ymas Heli, Messias, Tolimi, Elias, Ischiros, Athanatos, Imas . By these thy holie names, and by all other I doo call upon thee, and beseech thee O Lord Jesus Christ, by thy nativitie and baptisme, by thy crosse and passion, by thine ascension, and by the comming of the Holie-ghost, by the bitternesse of thy soule when it departed from thy bodie, by thy five wounds, by the bloud and water which went out of thy bodie, by thy vertue, by the sacrament which thou gavest thy disciples the daie before thou sufferedst, by the holie trinitie, and by the inseparable unitie, by blessed Marie thy mother, by thine angels, archangels, prophets, patriarchs, and by all thy saints, and by all the sacraments which are made in thine honour, I doo worship and beseech thee, I blesse and desire thee, to accept these prayers, conjurations, and words of my mouth, which I will use. I require thee O Lord Jesus Christ, that thou give me thy vertue & power over all thine angels (which were throwne downe from heaven to deceive mankind) to drawe them to me, to tie and bind them, & also to loose them, to gather them togither before me, & to command them to doo all that they can, and that by no meanes they contemne my voice, or the words of my mouth; but that they obeie me and my saiengs, and feare me. I beseech thee by thine humanitie, mercie and grace, and I require thee Adonay, Amay, Horta, Vege dora, Mitai, Hel, Suranat, Ysion, Ysesy, and by all thy holie names, and by all thine holie he saints and she saints, by all thine angels and archangels, powers, dominations, and vertues, and by that name that Salomon did bind the divels, and shut them up, Elhrach, Ebanher, Agle, Goth, Ioth, Othie, Venoch, Nabrat, and by all thine holie names which are written in this booke, and by the vertue of them all, that thou enable me to congregate all thy spirits throwne downe from heaven, that they may give me a true answer of all my demands, and that they satisfie all my requests, without the hurt of my bodie or soule, or any thing else that is mine, through our Lord Jesus Christ thy sonne, which liveth and reigneth with thee in the unitie of the Holie-ghost, one God world without end.

Oh father omnipotent, oh wise sonne, oh Holie-ghost, the searcher of harts, oh you three in persons, one true godhead in substance, which didst spare Adam and Eve in their sins; and oh thou sonne, which diedst for their sinnes a most filthie disgraceful death, susteining it upon the holie crosse; oh thou most mercifull, when I flie unto thy mercie, and beseech thee by all the means I can, by these the holie names of thy sonne; to wit, A and Omega, and all other his names, grant me thy vertue and power, that I may be able to cite before me, thy spirits which were throwne downe from heaven, & that they may speake with me, & dispatch by & by without delaie, & with a good will, & without the hurt of my bodie, soule, or goods, &c: as is conteined in the booke called Annulus Salomonis.

Oh great and eternall vertue of the highest, which through disposition, these being called to judgement, Vaicheon, Stimulamaton, Esphares,Tetragrammaton, Olioram, Cryon irion , Esytion, Existion, Eriona, Onela, Brasim, Noym, Messias, Soter, Emanuel, Sabboth  Sabaoth , Adonay, I worship thee, I invocate thee, I imploie thee with all the strength of my mind, that by thee, my present praiers, consecrations, and conjurations be hallowed: and whersoever wicked spirits are called, in the vertue of thy names, they may come togither from everie coast, and diligentlie fulfill the will of me the exorcist. Fiat, fiat, fiat, Amen.

(5) This kind of blasphemy and swearing constitutes the worst kind of refuse and dregs of the earth, and punishment of these profane magi is well deserved.

**END**

# DE SEPTEM SECUNDEIS

# DE SEPTEM SECUNDEIS

**JOHN TRITEMIUS**

**ON THE SEVEN SECONDARY CAUSES OF THE HEAVENLY INTELLIGENCES, GOVERNING THE ORBS UNDER GOD.**

**TRANSLATED 1647, BY WILLIAM LILLY**

# DEDICATION:

## TO THE EMPEROR MAXIMILIAN

Renowned Caesar, it is the opinion of very many of the Ancients, that this inferious World by ordination of the first *Intellect* (which is God) is directed and ordered by *Secundarian Intelligences,* to which opinion *Conciliator Medicorum* assents, saying, that from the Original or first beginning of heaven and earth, there were seven spirits appointed as Presidents to the seven planets.

Of which number every one of those rules the world 354 years, and four months in order.

To this Position, many, and they most learned men, have afforded their consent; which opinion of theirs *myself* not affirming, but delivering, do make manifest to your most sacred Majesty.

# DE SEPTEM SECUNDEIS

The first Angel or Spirit of *Saturn* is called *Orifiel*, to whom God committed the government of the World from the beginning of its Creation; who began his government the 15th day of the month of *March*, in the first year of the World, and it endured 354 years and 4 months.

*Orifiel* notwithstanding is a name appertaining to his Office, not his Nature. Attributed to the Spirit in regard of his action, under his dominion men were rude, and cohabited together in desert and uncouth places, living after the manner of Beasts. This does not need any manner of proof from me, since its so manifest out of the Text of Genesis.

The second Governor of the World is *Anael* the Spirit of *Venus*, who after *Orifiel* began to rule according to the influence of this Planet, in the year of the world 354. the fourth month, that is, the 24 day of the month of *June*, and he ruled the world 354 years, and 4 months, until the year from the Creation of the world 708, as it would appear to any that shall Calculate the Age thereof.

Under the Regiment of this Angel, men began to be more Civilized, built Houses, erected Cities, discovered the Manufacturing Arts: the Art of Weaving, Spinning, and Cloathing, and many such like as these, and indulged themselves plentifully with the pleasures of the flesh, took unto themselves fair women for their wives, neglected God, Receded in many things from their natural simplicity; they discovered Sports, and Songs, sang to the Harp, and did excogitate whatsoever did belong to the worship and purpose of *Venus*. And this wantonness of life by mankind continued until the flood, receiving the Arguments of its pravity ever since.

*Zachariel* the Angel of *Jupiter,* began to govern the world in the year of the Creation of Heaven and Earth 708 the eighth month, that is, the 25 day of the month of *October,* and he regulated the World 354 years, 4 months, until the year of the worlds Creation 1063, inclusively. Under whose moderation, men first of all began to usurp Dominion over one another, to exercise Hunting, to make Tents, to adorn their bodies with several garments: and there arose a great Division between good and evil men; the Pious invocating God, such as *Enoch,* whom the Lord translated to Heaven' the wicked running after the snares and pleasant allurements of the Flesh.

Men also under the Dominion of this *Zachariel* began to live more civilly, to undergo the Laws and Commands of their Elders, and were reclaimed from their former fierceness. Under his rule *Adam* the first man died, leaving to all posterity an assured Testimony, that it was certain that we all must die, eventually.

Various Arts and Inventions of men did about this time first appear and manifest themselves, as Historians have more clearly expressed.

The fourth Rector of the World was *Raphael,* the Spirit of *Mercury* which began in the year of the Creation of Heaven and Earth 1063 the 24th day of *February,* and he reigned 354 years 4 months, and his Government continued until the year of the World 1417 and fourth month. In these times writing was first discovered, and letters resembling Trees and Plants, which notwithstanding afterwards and in process of time, received a more graceful shape, and the Nations varied or changed the Face of their Characters according to their own fancy. The use of Musical Instruments, under the time and rule of *Raphael,* began to be multiplied, and Commerce or Exchange between men was now first invented: A presumptuous, rude and simple Audacity in these times begot

Navigation or the manner of Sailing from one place to another, and many such like things in one kinde or other, etc.

The fifth *Gubernator* of the World was *Samuel* the Angel of *Mars*, who began the 26 day of the month of *June* in the year of the World 1417, and swayed the rule of this World 354 years 4 months, until the year of the World 1771 and the eighth month, under whose Empire and Government men imitated the nature of *Mars*, also under the Dominion of this Angel, the Universal deluge of waters happened *Anno Mundi* 1656, as evidently it appears by History out of *Genesis*. And its to be observed, what the ancient Philosophers have delivered, that so oft as *Samuel* the Angel of *Mars* is ruler of the World, so often there arises notable alterations of Monarchy. Religions and sects vary, Laws are changed, Principalities and Kingdoms are transferred to Strangers, which we may easily find out in order by the perusal of Histories.

Notwithstanding *Samuel* does not immediately, in the very beginning or entrance of his Dominion, manifest the disposition of his behaviour or custom: but when he has exceeded the middle time of his *Gubernation*, which very thing is likewise to be understood concerning the Angels of the other Planets, (as it may be manifested from Histories) all which send down their influence according to the Proprieties of the natures of their Stars, and operate upon the inferior bodies of this World.

The sixth Governor of the World is *Gabriel* the Angel of the Moon, who began after *Samuel* the Angel of *Mars* had finished his course upon the 28 day of the month of *October* in the year of the World 1771 and eighth month: and he ordered the affairs of the World 354 years and 4 months, until the year of the World 2126. Again in these times men were multiplying, and built many Cities, and we must note: that the Hebrews affirm that the General deluge, was *Anno Mundi* 1656 - under the moderation of *Mars*: But the Septuagint interpreters, *Isidorus* and *Beda* confirm the Deluge to be in the year of the World 2242 under the Regiment of Gabriel, the Angel of the Moon, which seems to me by Multiplication to be consistent with the truth, but to express my further conception hereof, is not the work of this present discourse.

*Michael* the Angel of the Sun was the 7th Ruler of the World, who began the 24th of *February*, in the year of the World according to common computation 2126, and he governed the world 354 years and four months, until the year of the age of the world 2480 and four months.

Under the Dominion of the Angel of the Sun even as Histories consent with truth, Kings began first to be amongst Mortal men, of whom *Nimrod* was the first, that with an ambitious desire of Sovereignty, did Tyrannize over his Companions.

The worship of several Gods by the foolishness of men, was now instituted, and they began to adore their petty Princes as Gods.

Sundry Arts also about this time were invented by men; to wit, the Mathematics, Astronomy, Magic, and that worship, which formerly was attributed to the one and only God, began now to be given to diverse Creatures: the knowledge of the true God, by little and little, through the superstition of men, became forgotten.

About these times Architecture was discovered, and men began to use more policy both in their civil institutions, and manners, or customs of living.

From this time, the eighth time in order, again *Orifiel* the Angel of *Saturn* began to govern the World on the 26th day of the month of *June*, in the year from the beginning of the world 2480 and the fourth month; and he continued his government of the world this second return, 354 years and four months, until the year of the world 2834. and eight months. Under the regulation of this Angel, the Nations were multiplied, and the earth was divided into Regions; many Kingdoms were instituted; the Towel of *Babel* was built, the confusion of Tongues then fell out, men were dispersed into every part of the earth, and men began to Till, and Manure the earth more acurately, to ordain Fields, sow Corn, plant Vineyards, to dig up Trees, and to provide with greater diligence, what ever was more convenient for their food, and rainment.

From that time forward, first of all, amongst men, the discerning of Nobility begun to be noticed; which was, when men in their manner of living, and in wisdom excelled the rest of men, undertaking Trophies of glory from the great ones of the earth, as rewards for their merits: From this time, first of all, the whole world began to come into the knowledge of men, while everywhere the Nations were being multiplied, many Kingdoms arose, and various differences of tongues followed.

The ninth time in order and course, *Anael*, the Angel of *Venus* began again to sway the world the 29th day of *October* in the year of the Creation of Heaven and earth 2834 and the 8th month: and he presided 354 years and four months, until the year of the world 3189.

In these times men forgetting the true God, began to honour the dead, and to worship their Statues for God, the Error which infected the World for more than two thousand years. Men now devised curious and costly Ornaments, for better trimming, and adorning their bodies, found out diverse kindes of Musical Instruments. Again, men prosecuted too much the lust and pleasures of the flesh, instituting, and dedicating Statues and Temples to their Gods. Witchcraft, and Incantations in these times were first excogitated by *Zoroaster* King of the *Bactrians* (and diverse others as well as he) whom *Ninus* King of *Assyria* overcame in War.

In order the tenth time *Zachariel* the Angel of *Jupiter*, again began to rule the world the last day of *February*, in the year of the building, or framing the heaven and earth, 3189. And he moderated according to his custom and manner 354 years, and four months, until the year of the world 3543 and four months.

These were joyful times, and might truly be called golden, wherein there was plenty of all manner of useful things, which much conducive for the increase of mankind, giving thereby exceeding beauty and adornment to the things of this World.

In like manner about this time, God gave to *Abraham* the *Law* of *Circumcision*; and first of all promised the *Redemption* of *Mankind* by the *Incarnation* of his only begotten Son.

Under the Government of this Angel, the Patriarchs, the first *Founders* of *Justice*, were famous, and the righteous were divided from the ungodly, by their own proper indeavor and consent.

About these times in *Arcadia*, *Jupiter* grew famous, who was styled also *Lisania*, the Son of Heaven and God, a King, who first of all gave Laws to the Arcadians, made them very civil in their manners and behaviour, taught them the worship of God, erected them Temples, instituted Priests, procured many advantagious benefits for mankind, for which his so great benefits, he was by them termed *Jupiter*, and after his death was accounted for as a *Deity* or a God.

He had his Original from the sons of *Heber, viz. Gerar*, as ancient Histories do record to posterity.

*Prometheus* also the son of *Atlas* is reported under the Government of this Angel to have made Men; only, because of their rudeness and ignorance, he made them wise and knowing, humane, courteous, accomplished in learning and manners: he made Images by Art to move of themselves.

He first found out the use of the Ring, Scepter, Diadem, and all kingly ornaments.

In or about these times other jovial men excelled; *men* most wise, and *women* also, who by their own understanding delivered many profitable inventions to mankind; who being dead, for the greatness of their wisdom, were reputed as Gods: viz. *Photoneus*, who first of all instituted amongst the Greeks, Laws, and judgements, as also, *Sol, Minerva, Ceres, Serapis* amongst the *Aegyptians*, and very many besides.

In order the 11th time, *Raphael* the Angel of *Mercury* again undertook the ordering of the world the first day of the month of *July*, in the year of the world 3543 and the fourth month; he continued in his Commands 354 years, and four months, until the year of the Creation of heaven and earth 3897 and 8 months.

Verily in these times, as it evidently appears from the Histories of the Ancients, men more earnestly applied themselves to the study of wisdom, amongst whom the last learned and most eminent men, were *Mercurius, Bacchus, Omogyius, Isis, Inachus, Argus, Apollo, Cecrops*, and many more, who by their admirable inventions, both profited the world then, and in posterity since.

Several Superstitions also about these times, concerning the worship of their Idols were instituted by men.

Sorceries, Incantations, and Arts of framing Diabolical Images, were now in a marvelous manner increased, and whatsoever either of subtlety, or wit, that could possibly be attributed to the invention, or cunning of *Mercury* about these times, exceedingly increased.

*Moses* the wisest Commander of the Hebrews, expert in the knowledge of many things and Arts, a Worshipper of the one, only true God, deliverd the people of *Israel* from the slavery of the *Aegyptians*, and procured their liberty.

About this time *Janus* first of all reigned in *Italy*, after him *Saturnus*, who instructed his people to fat their grounds with soil or dung, and was accounted or esteemed for a God.

Near these times *Cadmus* found out the Greek Letters, or Characters, and *Carmentis*, the daughter of *Evander*, the Latin.

God Omnipotent, under the Government of this *Raphael*, the Angel of *Mercury*, delivered by the hands of *Moses*, to his people a Law in writing, which gave manifest testimony of our Saviour *Jesus Christ*, his future birth and nativity to be born in the flesh.

Here arose in the World a wonderful diversity of Religions: During these times, here flourished many *Sybills, Prophets, Diviners, Soothsayers*, or such as used inspection into the entrails of Beasts, *Magitians*, or *Wise-men, Poets*, as *Sybilla, Erythraea*, she of the Isle of *Delphos*, she whom we call the Phrygian, because she lived in *Phrygia* with the rest.

Again in order the twelfth time, *Samuel* the Angel of *Mars*, began to exercise his Dominion upon the world, the second day of the month of *October*, in the year of the world 3897 and the eighth month, and his time of ruling, was 354 years, and four months from then, until the year 4252 under whose Empire and rule, was that great and most famous Destruction of *Troy* in *Asia* the less: as also an admirable mutation, and alteration of *Monarchy*, and many Kingdoms together with new institutions, or moldings of many Cities, as *Paris, Monunce, Carthage, Naples*, and very many besides these.

Many new Kingdoms were newly erected, or now had their first beginning, as that of the *Lacedemonians, Corinthians, Hebrews*, and many others.

Here in these times all over the whole world, there were very great wars, and Battles of Kings and Nations, and several alterations of Empires.

The Venetians from this time, compute and reckon the original both of their people and City from the Trojans.

And its observable that very many other Nations, as well in *Europe* as in *Asia*, pretend to have taken their original from the Trojans, to whom I thought good to give so much credit, as they themselves were able to persuade me was truth, upon sufficient testimony and proof.

The Arguments they produce concerning their Nobility and Antiquity are frivolous, being desirous to magnify themselves openly, as if there were no People, or Nation in *Europe*, before the Destruction of *Troy*, or as if there had been no Pesant, or Clown amongst the Trojans.

Under the moderation also of this Planet, *Saul* was made first King of the Jews, after him *David*, whose son King *Salomon*, built in *Jerusalem* the Temple of the true God, the most famous and glorious of the whole world: from hence the Spirit of God illustrating, and enlightening his Prophets with a more ample illumination of his grace, they did not only foretel of the future incarnation of our Lord and Saviour, but also many other things, as holy Scriptures do testify, amongst whom were Nathan son of King *David, Gad, Asaph, Achias, Semeias, Asarias, Anan*, and many others.

*Homer* the Greek Poet, writer of *Troys* Destruction, *Dares, Phrygius, Dyctis Cretensis*, who were themselves at the razing, and sacking thereof, and have likewise described it, are supported to have been alive near about these times.

The thirteenth time in order, *Gabriel* the Spirit of the Moon, again undertook the ordering of this world the 30th day of *January* in the year from the beginning of the *Universe* 4252, and he presided in his Government 354 years, 4 months, until the year of the World 4606, and the fourth month.

In this time many Prophets were famous and excelled amongst the Jews, videlicet: *Helias, Heliseus, Micheas, Abdias*, with many others: There were many alterations of the Kingdom of the Jews: *Lycurgus* gave Laws and Ordinances to the *Lacedemonians, Capetus, Sylvius. Lyberius Sylvius, Romulus Sylvius, Procas Sylvius, Numitor*, Kings of *Italy* flourished, during the moderation of this spirit: more Kingdoms also had their Original or foundation under him, as those of the *Lydians, Medes, Macedonians, Spartans*, and others: the Monarchy of *Assyrians* under *Sardanapalus* now ended. And in like manner the Kingdom of the *Macedonians* was consumed, or worn out.

Sundry laws are imposed on men, the worship of the true God is neglected, and the Religion of false Gods is propagated too much: the City of Rome is built under the Dominion of this Spirit, in the year 1484, which year in order, was the 239 of the Angel *Gabriel*, the Kingdom of the *Sylvans* in *Italy* now ended, and that of *Rome* began in these times, *Thales, Chilon, Periander, Cleobulus, Bias, and Pittacus*, the seven wise men of Greece flourished, and from thence Philosophers and Poets came into request. At *Rome, Romulus* the first founder of the City reigned 37 years being a Fratricide and a stirrer up of Sedition. After whom *Numa Pompilius* continued that Kingdom in peace for a full 42 years: he amplified the worship of the Gods, and lived in the time of *Hezekiah*, King of *Judea*. About the expiration of this Angel of the Moon his government: *Nebuchadonozor* King of *Babylon*, took *Jerusalem*, and destroyed *Zedechiah* the King and carried away all the people Captive.

*Jeremiah* the Prophet was now famous, who fore-told this destruction, as also their future delivery from *Babylon*.

When *Gabriel* had finished his course, again *Michael,* Angel of the Sun, assumed the 14th government of the World, who began the first day of the month of *May,* in the year of the World, 4606 and the fourth month, and ruled the World according to his own order 354 years, until the year of the Worlds Creation, 4960 and the eighth month.

In the time of this Angels moderation *Evil Merodach* King of *Babylon,* restored both their Liberty and King to the people of the Jews, according to the direction of the Angel *Michael,* who as *Daniel* wrote, stood for the Nation of the Jews, unto whom they were committed by God.

In these times, likewise, the Monarchy of the Kingdom of the Persians began, whose first King *Darius*: and the second *Cyrus* brought to nothing or utterly ruined, that most powerful Kingdom of *Babylon* in the days of *Balthazar,* (as *Daniel* and the Prophets had predicted.)

In these times *Sybilla Cumana* was much spoken of, and grew famous; who brought 9 books to *Tarquinius Priscus* the King to be bought for a certain price; in which were contained the reason, order, and succession of future Advisements, of the whole commonwealth of the Romans. But when the King refused to give her the price demanded, *Sybilla* (the King seeing it) burnt the three first books, demanding the same price for the other six; which when again he had denied to give her, she committed to be burnt three of those remaining, and would have done so by the rest; unless the King by persuasion and through the Councel of others, had not redeemed them from such consumption, giving the same price for the last three, for which he might have had the whole nine.

Moreover the Romans having abrogated Government by Kings constituted two Consuls to reign every year.

*Phalaris* the Tyrant in these times occupied *Sicilia: Magique* or natural Philosophy was also, in these times, highly esteemed amongst the Kings of *Persia*.

*Pythagoras* the Philosopher, and very many others, flourished amongst the *Greeks;* the Temple and City of *Jerusalem* was now rebuilt.

*Esdras* the Prophet repaired the books of *Moses,* burned by the *Chaldeans*; who were also called *Babylonians*, and committed them to memory for example. *Xerxes* King of the *Persians* brought his Army against the *Greeks*, but had no success therein. The City of *Rome* is taken, burned, and destroyed, by the *Gaules*; the Capitol only preserved by a Goose, stirring up the weary Champions. The *Athenians* had eminent wars in these times: *Socrates et Plato* Philosophers lived now.

The Romans lessened the power of their Consuls, instituted *Tribunes et Aedils,* and were also about these times involved in many calamities: *Alexander* the great after the expiration of the rule of *Michael,* reigned in *Macedonia,* destroyed the Monarchy of the *Persians* in *Darius*: conquered all *Asia,* and annexed it with part of *Europe* to his own Empire.

He lived 33 years, reigned 12 after whose death infinite wars and many mischiefs followed, and his Monarchy became divided amongst four.

Now amongst the Jews, first of all, they began to contend for the Priesthood: the Kingdom of *Syria* began.

After the Spirit of *Michael* had finished his course, then the 15th time in order, *Orifiel* the Angel of *Saturn,* the third time assumed the regulating of this World, during the last day of the month of *September,* in the year from the building of the *Universe,* 4960 and the eighth month: and he ruled in Chief 354 years, 4 months, until the year of the World 5315. Under whose moderation, the *Punick* war began between the *Romans* and *Carthaginians*: the City of *Rome* was almost wholly consumed by fire and water. The Brazen Molten Image called *Colossus,* in length one hundred and twenty six feet, fell down, being shaken by an earthquake. At, or near this time the City of *Rome* enjoyed peace one year after the *Punick* War: which Common-wealth had never been without War in 440 years before.

*Jerusalem* together with the Temple is burnt and destroyed by *Antiochus* and *Epiphanes*, the History of the *Machabees* and their Wars were now acted.

In these times *Carthage* 606 years after its first foundation is destroyed, and burned continually by the space of 17 whole days. In *Sicilia* seventy thousand slaves made a Conspiracy against their Masters.

Many *Prodigies* in these times were beheld in *Europe*; tame domestic cattle fled to the Woods, it rained blood, a fiery Ball shined, appeared, and glistered out of heaven with great noise and crackling. *Mithridates* King of *Pontus*, and *Armenia* held Wars with the *Romans* over 40 years. The Kingdom of the Jews is restored, which had interruption 575 years from the time of *Zedechia* until *Aristobalus*. The people also of *Germany* called the *Theutines*, invaded the *Romans* and after many fights are overcome and one hundred and threescore thousand of them slain, besides innumerable others of them, who slew themselves and familiars under *Cajus* and *Mantius* the Consuls: notwithstanding this, many of the *Romans* were before this cut off by them: after which time, Civill Wars did much shake the *Romane* Common-wealth, which endured full 40 years. Three *Suns* appeared and were seen in *Rome*, but not long ere they were reduced into one.

A very few years succeeding, *Julius Cajus Caesar* usurped the government of the *Romans*, which *Octavius Augustus* after him amplified, and joyned *Asia, Africk* and *Europe* into one Monarchy he reigned 36 years by whom, or whose means God gave peace to the whole World: In the year from the building of the City 751. and of *Caesar Octavius Augustus* 42. and in the 245 year and eighth month, the 25 of *December*, of the government of the aforesaid *Orifiel* the Angel of *Saturne*: Iesus Christ the Son of God is born in *Bethelem* of *Iudea*, of *Mary* the Virgin. Note, how faire and wonderfull the Ordination of Divine providence is; for the World at first was created under the rule of *Saturn* his Angel

*Orifiel*: and mercifully redeemed, instaurated, and made new again under his third government; so that the great number and agreement of concurring Actions, may seem to administer no small beliefe to this manner of description, or setting forth, that this World is governed by the seaven Angels of the Planets: for in the first Gubernation of *Orifiel*, there was one only Monarchy of the whole World, under his second (as we mentioned before) it was divided amongst many.

Again, during his third, (as is manifest) it was reduced into one, although, if we consider or measure time aright, it is manifest also that in the second government of *Orifiel*, there was but one only Monarchy, when the Tower of *Babel* was built. From this time forward the Kingdom of the Jews was quite taken away, and the sacrifice of meat-offerings ceased, nor shall liberty be restored to the Jews before the third Revolution of the Angel *Michael*, and this shall be after the Nativity of Christ, in the year 1880, in the eighth month, videlecit In the year of the World 7170. and eight months. Many of the Jews in those times, and of the Gentiles also, shall embrace Christian Religion, most plain and simple men preaching the word of God, whom no human institution, but a divine spirit hath inspired. The World shall then be brought to its first innocency of its simplicity, the Angel of *Saturne Orifiel* governing the World every where.

Celestial things are mixed with earthly, many of the Christians, for that faith which they Preached, shall be slaughtered by the rulers of this World. About the ending of the Moderation of *Orifiel*, *Jerusalem* is destroyed by the *Romans*, and the *Jews* are dispersed into every Nation, there being massacred of them eleven hundred thousand, and four score thousand sold for slaves, the residue of them fled; and so the *Romans* wholly destroyed *Judea*.

After *Orifiel* had finished his government, *Anael* the Angel of *Venus*, the sixteenth in order, the third time reassumed his Regiment of the World: the last day of *January*, in the year of creating the Heaven and the Earth 5315, but from the year of the birth of Christ 109, and he regulated the affairs of the World 354 years and 4 months, until the years of the World 5669 and 4 months, but of the Nativity of our Savior Jesus Christ in the flesh 463. And it's remarkable, that almost during the whole rule of this

*Anael* the Angel of *Venus*, the Church of Christians flourished in her persecutions, and prevailed; many thousands, of men being Butchered for the Faith of Christ. Moreover in these times, very many Heresies began to be broached in the Church, which were not extinguished, but only after some time, and with labour and the blood of good men.

Many men were eminent about these times in all manner of learning, and such as were learned and Eloquent Diviners, Astronomers, Physitians, Orators, Historiographers, and men of like quality, not only amongst the *Gentiles*, but *Christians*. At length the persecution of *Infidels* ceased, after that *Constantine Caesar* the great, had assumed the Christian faith, in the year of the World 5539, after the middle of the Government of the aforesaid *Anael* the Angel of *Venus*. Although those professing the Religion and faith of Iesus Christ in some measure were now and then disturbed and molested by the Ungodly; Yet notwithstanding the peace of the Church did remain free from molestation a long time.

From this time forward, Mankind which from the time of *Ninus* the King, for almost the space of two thousand and three hundred years, had most miserably gone astray about the worship of Idols, was now revoked mercifully to the knowledge of one only God.

Various Arts of Subtlety in these times were augmented, and had increase and reputation according to their convenience to the nature of *Venus*.

For the manners of men are changed with the time, and the inferior bodies are disposed according to the influence of the superiors.

The mind of man (verily) is free, and receives not the influence of the Stars, unless it does too much commaculate his affection, by inclining its self with the commerce which it has with the body. For the Angels who are the movers of the Orbs, neither destroy nor subvert any thing, which nature it self has constituted or framed.

A Comet of unwonted and unusual greatness preceded the death of *Constantine*.

The *Arrian* Heresie in many Countries disturbed the holy Church.

Toward the end of this Angels Government, in the time of *Julianus Caesar*, Crosses appeared in lines, and Crosses in the garments of men.

In *Asia* and *Palaestina* wars followed, Pestilences and Famine in those places where the Crosses appeared.

In these times also about the year of our Lord 360. the *Franks* or *Franconians* in *Germany* had their Originall; who afterwards wasting *Gallia*, gave the name unto it of *France*, having first overcome and conquered the people thereof. The description of *Francia* in greatness is long and wide, or of great circuit, whose *Metropolis Moguntia* sometimes was; now truly and only *Herbipolis*.

The *Bavarians, Suevians*, the people of *Rhine, Saxons, Thuringers*, this day do occupy a great part of *France* in *Germany*, under jurisdiction of the *Papacy* in some places. Moreover in the 280 year of the Gubernation of this Angel *Anael*, the *Roman Empire* began to decline, while the City was taken and burned by the *Goths* the *Imperial* seat being first translated into *Greece* under *Constantine*, which was very mischievously done, and the only cause of the declining of that whole Monarchy: for near the determination of this Angel *Anael* his Regiment, there did arise *Radigifus, Alaricus, Atholfus*, Kings of the *Gothes*: Also after this *Genserick* of the *Vandals* and *Attilas* of the *Hunns* who running all over *Europe*, did most miserably tear the Empire assunder, as is evident in these Histories.

When *Anael* the Angel of *Venus* had finished his Regiment, then *Zachariel* the Spirit of *Jupiter* reassumed the Universal Government of this World the seventh time, the first day of *June*, in the year of the World 5669 and the fourth month, but in the year of our Lord and Saviour Jesus Christ 463 and four months; and governed in his turn 354 years and four months until the year of the World 6023 and the eighth month: but of our Lord God 817.

Many men in these times out of their affection to Christian Philosophy, took themselves to live in the Wilderness: many Prodigies appeared, Comets, Earthquakes, it rained blood.

Merlin born in *Tumbe,* predicted wonderful things in the beginning or entrance of this Angels Government.

*Arthurus* who commonly is called *Arthur,* the most glorious King of Great Britain, who overcame the *Barbarians,* restored peace to the Church, went away conqueror in many battles: propagated the Faith of Christ, subdued to his dominion all *Gallia, Norway, Denmark,* and many other Provinces. He was the most glorious of all Kings that lived in his time, who after many famous actions performed, never more appearred, being expected to return by the Britains for many years, of whom in times past many praise-worthy songs were published by the Bards of that people of wonderful Poets; for whilest he reigned, *England* was in its most flourishing condition, unto whom thirteen kingdoms were subject.

In or near these times the several Orders of *Monks* began to multiply in the Church of God: *Theodoric* King of *Gothes* being an Arian possessed all *Italy,* and murdered *Boetius* their Consul.

All manner of Estates were full of perturbation, as well as the Empire as Church affairs, or Church and Common-wealth were now in great distress.

*Zenon* and *Anastasius, Arrian* Emperors in the East, *Theodoric* and his successors in *Italy, Honorius* King of the *Vandalls* in *Affrica* excercised no small Tyranny.

*Clodoucus* King of *France* at length in Gallia being turned Christian, both overcame the *Gothes,* and restored peace in many places, though not in every Country and Kingdom.

In the time of *St. Benedict,* and year of Christ 500, or thereabouts, in the beginning of the government of this Angel *Zachariel* the Spirit of *Jupiter,* whose spirit's property it is, to change Empires and Kingdoms, which was done in this Revolution, histories manifoldly declared; and what himself could not perform, he ordained *Raphael* the Angel of *Mercury*, his successor, to perfect in *Charles* King of *French*-men.

Many Kingdoms came to their periods under these 350 years both of the *Gothes, Vandalls, Burgundians, Lumbards, Thuringers, Almains, Bavarians,* and very many besides.

*Justinianus* the Emperor first of all about these times beautified the Common-wealth very deservedly with his Laws.

Many gallant and most admirable men flourished under *Zachariel*.

*Justinianus* built the Temple of *St. Sophia* in *Constantinople,* consisting of 400 Towers. The Empire is divided and made Bi-partite, and ever and anon is more and more oppressed with mischiefs.
Many signs in heaven appeared about these times, as is easily collected from Histories.

*Cosdroes* king of the Persians took *Jerusalem,* whom *Heraclius* the Emperour afterward slew.

*Mahomet* the *Arabian* in these times about the year of Christ 600 introduced the Sect of *Sarazens,* by which Sect the Roman Empire in *Asia* is now quite extinguished.

*Dagobert* King of *France* slew the English, at that time called *Saxons* (whom in battle he overcame). Its remarkable, that by little and little Christianity about these times began to fail in *Asia* and *Affrick,* upon entrance of the Sect of the *Sarasins* therein, which now had almost poisoned the whole world.

About the years of our Lord God 774. Crosses appeared in the garments of men, and not long after the Roman Empire is divided, a translation of the *Monarchy* being made to *Charles* who was of the Frankes Nation in Germany, who preserved the Empire and Church from perishing, and fought many famous battles.

The name of *Western Galls,* or *Westphalians* in *Saxony* after his victory first had its beginning.

In the 18th place after finishing the rule of *Zachariel*, the Angel of *Jupiter*, *Raphael* the spirit of *Mercury* undertook the disposing of this worlds affaires, the third time, the second day of *November* in the year of the Creation of the World, 6023 in eighth month, and he swayed the scepter of the World 354 years and four months, until the years of the world 6378 and of our Lord God 1171.

In the first beginning of this revolution of *Raphael* the Angel of *Mercury*, the Monarchy of the Roman Empire (as we mentioned before) was translated to *Charles* the great.

After *Charles* his son *Lodowick* ruled 25 years, who being dead, his sons contending amongst themselves, did again extenuate the strength of the Empire.

The Normans harrowed *France: Rome* is twice scourged by the *Saracens*: under *Lodowick* the second it rained blood from Heaven in *Italy*, by the space of three whole days.

In *Saxony*, a certain village with all its buildings, and inhabitants was in a moment swept away by an horrible gaping or opening of the earth.

About the year of our Lord God 910, there were many great motions in *Italy*, and *Italy* fell from the Empire of the Franks or Franconians, and ordained proper kings for themselves of their own election; the first whereof was *Berengarius* the Duke of *Fonolivium*, after whom seven in order succeeded, near upon fifty years, until the translation of the Empire unto the *Germans*: The first Emperor that was thereof was *Otho*, from which time the Empire began to be reformed; unto whom *Otho* his son, and his Nephew *Otho* after succeeded in the Empire, under whose Government the Hungarians are converted to the Christian Faith. But the third *Otho* dying without children, instituted after his death Electors of the Empire in the year of Christianity 1002. even as they remain to this present day.

*Jerusalem* is again taken by the *Saracens*: many strange sights are seen in the air, in the Heavens, in the Earth and sea, and in waters: But *Otho* the third being dead, *Henry* the first by election of the Princes succeeded, reigned 20 years, who founded the Church of

*Bamburg*, and dying a Virgin, together with his wife *Kunigunda* he shone gloriously in miracles; after whom *Conrade*, first Duke of the Francks is chosen, and ruled 20. years.

*Godfrey* Earl of *Bullen* also recovered the holy Land, and City of *Jerusalem* from the hands of the Infidels.

Before the end of this Revolution many signs and Prodigies were seen, and a little time after the Nation of the *Tartars* exceeded the bounds of their own Country, and did many mischiefs to the Empire of *Rome*.

There was Famine, Pestilence, Earthquakes in the Empire: Three suns were seen in the East, and as many Moons. In the year of our Lord God 1153. *Frederick* first called *Barbarossa* began to reign, and ruled 33 years, the beginning of whose Government was in the 336th year of *Raphael*: He did many noble exploits, and enlarged the strength of that Empire, performed sundry wars with great success, in whose ninth year the *Egians* and *Lituotrians* were converted to the Faith of Christ.

*Samael* the Angel of *Mars* in order, the nineteenth time came to accept the Gubernation of the universal world, it being now his third return, and this he did the third day of *March, Anno Mundi*, 6378 and he regulated *mundane* affaires 354 years and four months, until the years of the World 6732 and four months; and of our Lord God 1525, under whose predominancy many wars were all over the whole world, by which means infinite thousands of men perished, and sundry Kingdoms lost their former bounds: between *Frederick* the first Emperor and the Roman Nobility, many controversies arose, sundry great battels were fought, and many thousands of *Romans* perished.

The aforesaid *Frederick* did wholy subvert *Mediolanum: Leige* is destroyed, *Jerusalem* is again taken by the *Saracens*, the Empire of the *Tartarians* the greatest in the whole World about these times took its beginning, occasioned a very great plague in the World, nor yet do they cease.

After *Frederick*, *Henrie* his Son is elected Emperor. Who being dead, Schism confounds that Empire; under *Philip* and *Otho* many battles followed in the confines of *Germany, Argentine, Cullen, Liege, Wormes, Spires,* and all over the Kingdom. The sect of begging or Mendicant Friars began in these times, in the 40th year, or thereabouts of *Samael*: from whence it is most apparent, that all things are done by providence. The *Sarazens* fought many battels against the Christians in *Asia* and *Africk. Constantinople* is taken by the *Germans: Baldwin* Earl of *Flanders* is instituted Emperor. In *Almain* more then twenty thousand young men are drowned in the Sea by *Pyrats,* who seduced by a vain spirit, did give forth they would recover the holy land.

From *Spain* many shepherds or keepers of cattle united themselves together, coming to *Paris* dispoiling the clergy of their livelyhoods, the common people taking part with them, or being well pleased with it.
But when they extended their hands to take away the goods of the Layity, they were quite cut off and destroyed.

In the year of Christ 1212. *Frederick* the second is elected, he reigned 33 years, and did many acts against the Church. In the year 1238, an Eclipse and a continual Earthquake undid many thousands of men.

*Frisia* also by continual incursions of the sea, was almost wholly drowned, and there perished more then one hundred thousand of men and women.

The *Tartars* waste *Hungaria* and *Polonia, Armenia* the greater being first subdued, and many regions besides.

In the year of Christ 1244, a certain Jew digging in the ground at *Toledo* in *Spain,* found a book, in which it was written, In the third World Christ shall be born of the Virgin *Mary*, and shall suffer for the salvation of man, not long after the third World believing, shall be baptized.

It was the third Revolution of the Angel of *Saturn*, concerning which, what is spoken is intended: in the beginning of whose reign, Christ was born of a Virgin.

The Popes of *Rome* deposing *Frederick*, it is said the Empire was vacant 28 years, until the Election of *Rodolph* Count of *Habspurg*, constituting Kings by turns in the Intervals or vacancy. First *Henry* Count of *Schuvartzenburg* at *Thuring* by election of the Princes; then *William* Earle of *Holland*, *Conrade* the Son of *Frederick*, *Alfonsus* King of *Castile*, *Richard* Earl of *Cornwall*, brother to the King of *England*, many evils were multiplied upon the face of the Earth.

At or near this time about the year of our Lord God 1260. the Confederacy of the *Switzers* began, a small people in number, but have increased with the time, who have slain many of their Nobility, and being a Warlike people have banished and frighted away many others of their Nobles from their proper habitations, whose Common wealth is now known to all the people of *Germany*.

In the year of Christians 1273, *Rudolphus* of *Habspurg* is constituted Emperor by Election of the Princes. He reigned 18 years, the best of men, prudent in all manner of affairs, from whom afterwards descended all the Dukes of *Austria*. The *Tartarians* invading the Lands of Christians, *Constantinpole* and *Greece*, brought infinite damage to the Christians.

The *Saracens* occupied many Cities in *Asia*, killing and destroying more than four hundred thousand Christians: *Rudolphus* being dead, *Adolph* of *Nassaw* is elected King, he governed six years, whom *Albert* the son of *Rudolph*, afterwards overcame and slew in a fight neer *Wormes* and was chosen Imperator in the year of Christ 1298. He governed ten years and was slain by his brother's son. The Order of the Knights Templars by command of Pope *Clement* the fifth is destroyed, the Isle of *Rhodes* is recovered by Christians out of the hands of the *Sarazens*, after the War and siege thereof had continued four whole years. *Albertus* being slain by his Nephew; *Henry* is constituted the eighth Emperor, being Count of *Luxenburg*, who reigned 5 years; he being dead *Lodowick* the fourth of *Bavaria* reigned 32 years, beginning in the year 1315, unto whom the Popes of *Rome* gave a Crown. *Frederick* Duke of *Austria* opposes himself against *Lodowick*, but is overcome by him.

After *Lodowick, Charles* the fourth King of *Bohemia* is constituted Emperor; who converted the Bishoprick of *Prague* into an Archbishoprick; he reigned 31 years: there were most fearful Earthquakes. This *Charles* did institute many things in favour of the Princes Electors, concerning their Customs and Tallys, which were not formerly in use. *Gunther* Count of *Schuartzenburg* styled himself King, opposed *Charles* the Emperor, but prevailed nothing at all against him.

After *Charles,* his Son *Winceslaus* governed 22 years: after whom *Jodocus* Marques of *Moravia* succeeded, *Sigismund* Cozen *German* of *Winceslaus.*

*Winceslaus* was disposed, *Leopold* Duke of *Austria,* 8 Earls, and more then 4000 souldiers fighting against the *Switzers,* were all slain by them.

During the government of *Winceslaus* King of *Bohemia* Emperor: the Tenets of *John Huss* had their beginning. *Winceslaus* being deposed, *Rupert* Count *Palatine* of *Rhine*, and Duke of *Bavaria* was elected, and ruled 10. years. In the year of our Lord God 1369, the Christians engaged themselves in a war against the *Sarazens,* which succeeded poorly, by reason of the *French* mens' Arrogancy: because more then one hundred thousand chrisitans died in that war; besides such as were made Captives, amongst whom was *John* Duke of *Burgundy*, many were the wars of those times.

In the year of the World 1407 *Sigismund* is made Emperor, and governed 27 years: he endeavoured to waste and destroy the Kingdom of *Bohemia* thereby to extinguish Heresy, but it availed him little. The Kingdom of *France* is most grievously wasted and consumed by the *English* and *Burgundians: Sigismund* being departed this life, *Albert* Duke of *Austria, Sigismunds* son in Law, succeeded in the year of the Christians 1438. and only reigned two years, an admirable man and worthy of the Empire. He being deceased, *Frederick* the third Duke of *Austria*, the Son of *Ernestus,* by election of the Princes, is chosen Emperor: and reigned 56 years, a man of a Divine soul and peaceable conversation, who began to rule *Anno Dom.* 1440.

In the year of Christians 1453, *Constantinople* is taken of the *Turks* by Treachery of a certain *Genoway*, and a little after by degrees all *Greece* fell from their Christian faith. For a litle time after many Kingdoms and Provinces of the Christians were harrowed, wasted, and taken by the *Turks*. Many and most grievous wars the Christians had amongst themselves about this time, in *France, England, Saxony, Westphalia, Prusia, Flanders, Sweden,* and other places. In these times the Art of Printing was newly discovered, and invented at *Mogunce* the Metropolis of *Almain,* by a wonderful industry, and not without the special gift of the Deity.

In the year of Christ 1456, the *Turks* were overthrown in *Hungaria* by the faithful Christians, whereof many of them perished. The Pilgrimage of young men to Saint *Michael was wonderful.* There were Earthquakes in the Kingdom of *Naples,* and more then fourty thousand people perished thereby.

In the year of the World 1462 *Moruntia* is taken and spoiled being the Metropolis of the *Franconians* or *Francks* in *Germany*.

*Charles* Duke of *Burgundy* overcame the *Franconians* in *Anno* 1465. After that in 1467 he destroyed the cities *Dinant et Liege, An.* 1473. He entered *Gelderland*, and with much valour obtained it, and in like manner all the whole Dukedome of *Loraigne*.

A Comet during all the month of *January* 1472 appeared. *Charles* Duke of *Burgundy* not long besieged the Town of *Nussicum* one whole years' space, videlecit in or about 1474. which Magnanimous Prince was afterwards slain in war in the year 1467. The *Turks* took away from the Christians about these times, many of their cities, *Nigropont* in *Euboia,* the Kingdom of *Bosnia,* Dukedome of *Speta, Achaia, Mysia,* and more Kingdoms besides these in the *East*.

*Anno* 1476 a convocation of fools was in *Franconia* of *Germany* neer *Niclaushausen,* full of errors.

*Anno* 1480 the *Turks* besieged the *Rhodians* with a powerful Army but did not prevail; departing the same year from *Rhodes*, they took the city *Hydruntum,* more then twelve thousand Christians were slain there, only 22 soldiers escaped. The next year *Mahomet*

Emperor of the *Turks* died; to whom *Bajazet* his first born succeeded in the Kingdom, having reigned now at this present 27 years. In the year of Christ 1486, *Maximilian* the Son of *Frederick* was instituted King of *Romans* at *Franckford,* and saluted *Caesar* by *Julius* the Pope 1508, who instituted the Order of warfare of Saint *George* purposely against *Hereticks* and *Turks:* he brought the *Switzers* low by war, and even to this day makes war against the Rebellious *Sicambrians;* he will be fortunate against all such as break their Leagues or Covenants with him.

The King of *France* after his wonted manner, a constant persecutor of the Empire, is discovered to plot new devices against it. The Omnipotent protects those assigned to the Government of *Samael: Anno* 1508. the *Venetians* Rebels to the Empire of *Caesar,* are threatened with War and Banishment. Punishment of stubbornness will be the reward of an advised satisfaction. About the end of this third Revolution of *Samael,* the Image of alteration shall pass to the first and shall be the Perdition of many men for unless *Aries* be reduced again, (God assisting) (ad algos) there will be a translation of one Monarchy, or of some great Kingdom.

A strong sect of Religion shall arise, and be the overthrowing of the Ancient Religion.

It's to be feared, lest the fourth beast lose one head.

*Mars* first of all in the Government of *Samael* foretold the Flood, in his second return, the siege and destruction of Troy: in his third toward the end thereof will be found great want of unity: from matters preceding may be Judged what will or ought to succeed. This third Revolution of *Mars* shall not be consummated without Prophecy, and the institution of some new Religion, from this year of our Lord 1508. Here yet remains until the end of the Government of *Samael* 17 years wherein signs and figures shall be given, foreshowing the beginnings of evil. For in *Anno.* 1525, crosses were seen in the garments of men by the space of ten years before, what is past already shall shew their effects: but 13 years from hence being justly summoned away, you shall surrender your place to the (*non Intelligent*) you shall revive again far greater to me, after the *Fates* in the third; unless it is lawful that you obscure yourself in a cloud.

The twentieth time in order, *Gabriel* Angel of the Moon received the moderation of the World, in the year of the World 6732, in the fourth month, and fourth day of *June:* in the year of Christ 1525, and he shall regulate the world 354. years, and four months, until the year of the world 7086 and the eighth month, but of our Lord Christ 1879 and the 11th month.

## THE FUTURE SERIES OF THIS REVOLUTION REQUIRES PROPHECY

Most sacred *Caesar*, I have not written these things assertively, nor must we believe it by any means whatever with the injury of Orthodox Divinity.

There are some that, in these things, have supputed Lunar months, which if you hold fit to consent unto, then those things I have written must be varied.

I protest with my own proper hand, and confess with my own mouth, that in all these things delivered, I believe nothing, nor admit to anything, except what the Catholic Church holds: the rest, I refute and contemn as vain, feigned and superstitious.

### FINIS

*Joh. Trit.*

# DÆMONOLOGIE

# DÆMONOLOGIE

## KING JAMES the FIRST

*(1597)*

EDITED BY G. B. HARRISON

# INTRODUCTION

# INTRODUCTION

The Dæmonologie of King James, the Sixth of Scotland and First of England, was written, as the Royal author states in his Preface, to prove that 'the assautes of Sathan are most certainly practized, & that the instrumentes thereof, merits most severly to be punished.' Such a work has more than a passing interest. It gives the student of history and literature a brief and authoritative guide to the darker beliefs of our ancestors; there is, too, much to interest the theologian and the psychologist, whilst the philologist will find the book a mine of rare and curious phrases.

To the modern mind, after three centuries of scientific discovery, many of Epistemon's arguments will appear somewhat naïve, and, it must be confessed, that Philomathes, in his laudable efforts to draw out his companion's erudition, sometimes puts questions which are very inadequately answered. Our greater discernment and weaker faith will scarcely be convinced by the example: 'Thirdly, said not Samuell to Saull, that disobedience is as the sinne of Witch-craft? To compare to a thing that were not, it were too too absurd.' Still, given the implicit belief, the conclusions are not illogical. King James makes many shrewd observations, and the twentieth-century medium would probably confirm 'that there are twentie women giuen to that craft, where ther is one man.' The explanation would not, perhaps, be as readily accepted.

The Newes from Scotland, which is also included in this volume of the Bodley Head Quartos, claims to give a true account of a very notable witch trial wherein King James took a prominent part. The influence of the 'revelations' then made can clearly be seen in the Dæmonologie. Although at first sight the cruelty and barbarity of the whole business is revolting, it must not be put down as solely due to panic and terror. These poor women when their heads were 'thrawen with a rope according to the custom of that Country' were ready to confess anything, but the credulity of the judges was understandable after Agnis Sampson had drawn the King aside and 'declared vnto him the verye woordes which passed betweene the Kings Maiestie and his Queene at Vpslo in Norway the first night of their marriage, with their answere each to other.' Even a stouter hearted scholar would have found remarkable confirmation of his worst fears in this alarming revelation. Moreover, in destroying the Devil's ministers the King really thought that he was only carrying out his plain duty towards God.

Of King James himself one of the most vivid accounts is to be found in a letter of Sir John Harrington, describing an audience which he had with the King. 'Soon upon this, the Prince his Highnesse did enter, and in muche goode humour askede, "If I was cosen to lorde Haryngton of Exton?" I humblie repliede,--"His Majestie did me some honour in enquiringe my kin to one whome he had so late honourede and made a barone;" and moreover did adde, "wee were bothe branches of the same tree." The he enquyrede muche of lernynge, and showede me his owne in suche sorte, as made me remember my examiner at Cambridge aforetyme. He soughte muche to knowe my advances in philosophie, and utterede profounde sentences of Aristotle, and suche lyke wryters, whiche I had never reade, and which some are bolde enoughe to saye, others do not understand: but this I must passe by. The Prince did nowe presse my readinge to him parte of a canto in "Ariosto"; praysede my utterance, and said he had been informede of manie, as to my lernynge, in the tyme of the Queene. He asked me "what I thought pure witte was made of; and whom it did best become? Whether a Kynge should not be the best clerke in his owne countrie; and, if this lande did not entertayne goode opinion of his lernynge and wisdome?" His Majestie did much presse for my opinion touchinge the power of Satane in matter of witchcraft; and asked me, with much gravitie,--"if I did trulie understande, why the devil did worke more with anciente women than others?"'.

'More serious discourse did next ensue, wherein I wantede roome to continue, and sometime roome to escape; for the Queene was not forgotten, nor Davison neither. His Highnesse tolde me her deathe was visible in Scotlande before it did really happen, being, as he said, "spoken of in secrete by those whose power of sighte presentede to them a bloodie heade dancinge in the aire." He then did remarke muche on this gifte, and saide he had soughte out of certaine bookes a sure waie to attaine knowledge of future chances. Hereat, he namede many bookes, which I did not knowe, nor by whom written; but advisede me not to consult some authors which woulde leade me to evile consultations. I tolde his Majestie, "the power of Satan had, I muche fearede, damagede my bodilie frame; but I had not farther will to cowrte his friendshipe, for my soules hurt."--We nexte discoursede somewhat on religion, when at lengthe he saide: "Now, Sir, you have seen my wisdome in some sorte, and I have pried into yours. I praye you, do me justice in your reporte, and in good season, I will not fail to add to your understandinge, in suche pointes as I maye find you lacke amendmente." I made courtesie hereat, and withdrewe downe the passage, and out at the gate, amidst the manie varlets and lordlie servantes who stoode arounde.'

G. B. HARRISON.

# DÆMONOLOGIE

**IN FORME
OF A DIALOGUE,
DIUIDED INTO THREE BOOKES.
EDINBVRGH
PRINTED BY ROBERT WALDE-GRAUE
PRINTER TO THE KINGS MAJESTIE. AN. 1597
CUM PRIVILEGIO REGIO**

# THE PREFACE

## TO THE READER

THE fearefull aboundinge at this time in this countrie, of these detestable slaues of the Deuill, the Witches or enchaunters, hath moved me (beloued reader) to dispatch in post, this following treatise of mine, not in any wise (as I protest) to serue for a shew of my learning & ingine, but onely (mooued of conscience) to preasse / thereby, so farre as I can, to resolue the doubting harts of many; both that such assaultes of Sathan are most certainly practized, & that the instrumentes thereof, merits most severly to be punished: against the damnable opinions of two principally in our age, wherof the one called SCOT an Englishman, is not ashamed in publike print to deny, that ther can be such a thing as Witch-craft: and so mainteines the old error of the Sadducees, in denying of spirits. The other called VVIERVS, a German Phisition, sets out a publick apologie for al these craftesfolkes, whereby, procuring for their impunitie, he plainely bewrayes himselfe to haue bene one of that Profession. And for to make this treatise the more pleasaunt and facill, I haue put it in forme of a Dialogue, which I haue diuided into three bookes: The first spea- / king of Magie in general, and Necromancie in special. The second of Sorcerie and Witch-craft: and the thirde, conteines a discourse of all these kindes of spirits, & Spectres that appeares & trobles persones: together with a conclusion of the whol work. My intention in this labour, is only to proue two things, as I haue alreadie said: the one, that such diuelish artes haue bene and are.

The other, what exact trial and seuere punishment they merite: & therefore reason I, what kinde of things are possible to be performed in these arts, & by what naturall causes they may be, not that I touch every particular thing of the Deuils power, for that were infinite: but onelie, to speak scholasticklie, (since this can not bee spoken in our language) I reason vpon genus leauing species, and differentia to be comprehended therein. / As for example, speaking of the power of Magiciens, in the first book & sixt Chapter: I say, that they can suddenly cause be brought vnto them, all kindes of daintie disshes, by their familiar spirit: Since as a thiefe he delightes to steale, and as a spirite, he can subtillie & suddenlie inough transport the same. Now vnder this genus, may be comprehended al particulars, depending thereupon; Such as the bringing Wine out of a Wall, (as we haue heard oft to haue bene practised) and such others; which particulars, are sufficientlie proved by the reasons of the general. And such like in the second booke of Witch-craft in speciall, and fift Chap. I say and proue by diuerse arguments, that Witches can, by the power of their Master, cure or cast on disseases: Now by these same reasones, that proues their power by the / Deuil of disseases in generall, is aswell proued their power in speciall: as of weakening the nature of some men, to make them vnable for women: and making it to abound in others, more then the ordinary course of nature would permit. And such like in all other particular sicknesses; But one thing I will pray thee to obserue in all these places, where I reason vpon the deuils power, which is the diferent ends & scopes, that God as the first cause, and the Devill as his instrument and second cause shootes at in all these actiones of the Deuil, (as Gods hang-man:) For where the deuilles intention in them is euer to perish, either the soule or the body, or both of them, that he is so permitted to deale with: God by the contrarie, drawes euer out of that euill glorie to himselfe, either by the wracke of the wicked in his justice, or / by the tryall of the patient, and amendment of the faithfull, being wakened vp with that rod of correction. Hauing thus declared vnto thee then, my full intention in this Treatise, thou wilt easelie excuse, I doubt not, aswel my pretermitting, to declare the whole particular rites and secretes of these vnlawfull artes: as also their infinite and wounderfull practises, as being neither of them pertinent to my purpose: the reason whereof, is giuen in the hinder ende of the first Chapter of the thirde booke: and who likes to be curious in these thinges, he may reade, if he will here of their practises, BODINVS Dæmonomanie, collected with greater diligence, then written with judgement, together with their confessions, that haue bene at this time apprehened. If he would know what hath bene the opinion of the Auncientes, concerning their power: he shall see it wel descrybed by HYPERIVS, & HEMMINGIVS, two, late Germaine writers: Besides innumerable other neoterick Theologues, that writes largelie vpon that subject: And if he woulde knowe what are the particuler rites, & curiosities of these black arts (which is both vnnecessarie and perilous,) he will finde it in the fourth book of CORNELIVS Agrippa, and in VVIERVS, whomof spak. And so wishing my pains in this Treatise (beloued Reader) to be effectual, in arming al them that reades the same, against these aboue mentioned erroures, and recommending my goodwill to thy friendly acceptation, I bid thee hartely fare-well.

JAMES R.

# THE FIRST BOOKE

**DAEMONOLOGIE,**
**IN FORME**
**of ane Dialogue**

# CHAPTER I

## ARGVMENT

Proven by the Scripture, that these vnlawfull artes in genere, have bene and may be put in practise.

PHILOMATHES and EPISTEMON reason the matter.

PHILOMATHES.

I AM surely verie glad to haue mette with you this daye, for I am of opinion, that ye can better resolue me of some thing, wherof I stand in great doubt, nor anie other whom-with I could haue mette.

EPI. In what I can, that ye like to speir at me, I will willinglie and freelie tell my opinion, and if I proue it not sufficiently, I am heartely content that a better reason carie it away then.

PHI. What thinke yee of these strange newes, which now onelie furnishes purpose to al men at their meeting: I meane of these Witches?

EPI. Surelie they are wonderfull: And I think so cleare and plaine confessions in that purpose, haue neuer fallen out in anie age or cuntrey.

PHI. No question if they be true, but thereof the Doctours doubtes.

EPI. What part of it doubt ye of?

PHI. Even of all, for ought I can yet perceaue: and namelie, that there is such a thing as Witchcraft or Witches, and I would pray you to resolue me thereof if ye may: for I haue reasoned with sundrie in that matter, and yet could never be satisfied therein.

EPI. I shall with good will doe the best I can: But I thinke it the difficiller, since ye denie the thing it selfe in generall: for as it is said in the logick schools, Contra negantem principia non est disputandum. Alwaies for that part, that witchcraft, and Witches haue bene, and are, the former part is clearelie proved b the Scriptures, and the last by dailie experience and confessions.

PHI. I know Yee will alleadge me Saules Pythonisse: but that as appeares will not make much for you.

EPI. Not onlie that place, but divers others: But I marvel why that should not make much for me?

PHI. The reasones are these, first Yee may consider, that Saul[1] being troubled in spirit, and having fasted long before, as the text testifieth, and being come to a woman that was bruted to have such knowledge, and that to inquire so important news, he having so guiltie a conscience for his hainous offences, and specially, for that same vnlawful curiositie, and horrible defection: and then the woman crying out vpon the suddaine in great admiration, for the vncouth sicht that she alledged to haue sene, discovering him to be the King, thogh disguysed, & denied by him before: it was no wounder I say, that his senses being thus distracted, he could not perceaue hir faining of hir voice, hee being himselfe in an other chalmer, and seeing nothing. Next what could be, or was raised? The spirit of Samuel? Prophane and against all Theologie: the Diuell in his likenes? as vnappeirant, that either God would permit him to come in the shape of his Saintes (for then could

---

[1] 1. Sam. 28

neuer the Prophets in those daies haue bene sure, what Spirit spake to them in their visiones) or then that he could fore-tell what was to come there after; for Prophecie proceedeth onelie of G O D: and the Devill hath no knowledge of things to come.

EPI. Yet if Yee will marke the wordes of the text, ye will finde clearely, that Saul saw that apparition: for giuing you that Saul was in an other Chalmer, at the making of the circles & conjurationes, needeful for that purpose (as none of that craft will permit any vthers to behold at that time) yet it is evident by the text, that how sone that once that vnclean spirit was fully risen, shee called in vpon Saul. For it is saide in the text, that Saule knew him to be Samuel, which coulde not haue bene, by the hearing tell onely of an olde man with an mantil, since there was many mo old men dead in Israel nor Samuel: And the common weid of that whole Cuntrey was mantils. As to the next, that it was not the spirit of Samuel, I grant: In the proving whereof ye neede not to insist, since all Christians of whatso-ever Religion agrees vpon that: and none but either mere ignorants, or Necromanciers or Witches doubtes thereof. And that the Diuel is permitted at som-times to put himself in the liknes of the Saintes, it is plaine in the Scriptures, where it is said, that Sathan can trans-forme himselfe into an Angell of light[1]. Neither could that bring any inconvenient with the visiones of the Prophets, since it is most certaine, that God will not permit him so to deceiue his own: but only such, as first wilfully deceiues them-selves, by running vnto him, whome God then suffers to fall in their owne snares, and justlie permittes them to be illuded with great efficacy of deceit, because they would not beleeue the trueth (as Paul sayth). And as to the diuelles foretelling of things to come, it is true that he knowes not all things future, but yet that he knowes parte, the Tragicall event of this historie declares it, (which the wit of woman could never haue fore-spoken) not that he hath any prescience, which is only proper to God: or yet knows anie thing by loking vpon God, as in a mirrour (as the good Angels doe) he being for euer debarred from the fauorable presence & countenance of his creator, but only by one of these two meanes, either as being worldlie wise, and taught by an continuall experience, ever since the creation, judges by likelie-hood of thinges to come, according to the like that hath

---

[1] 2. Cor. 11. 14.

passed before, and the naturall causes, in respect of the vicissitude of all thinges; worldly: Or else by Gods employing of him in a turne, and so foreseene thereof: as appeares to haue bin in this, whereof we finde the verie like in Micheas propheticque discourse to King Achab¹. But to prooue this my first proposition, that there can be such a thing as witch-craft, & witches, there are manie mo places in the Scriptures then this (as I said before). As first in the law of God, it is plainely prohibited²: But certaine it is, that the Law of God speakes nothing in vaine, nether doth it lay curses, or injoyne punishmentes vpon shaddowes, condemning that to be il, which is not in essence or being as we call it. Secondlie it is plaine, where wicked Pharaohs wise-men imitated ane number of Moses miracles³, to harden the tyrants heart there by. Thirdly, said not Samuell to Saull, that disobedience is as the sinne of Witch-craft?⁴ To compare to a thing that were not, it were too too absurd. Fourthlie, was not Simon Magus, a man of that craft? And fiftlie, what was she that had the spirit of Python?⁵ beside innumerable other places that were irkesom to recite.⁶

---

[1] 1. King. 22.
[2] Exod. 22.
[3] Exod. 7&8.
[4] 1. Sam. 15.
[5] Acts. 8.
[6] Acts. 16.

# CHAPTER II

## ARGV.

What kyndie of sin the practizers of these vnlawfull artes committes. The division of these artes. And quhat are the meanes that allures any to practize them.

PHILOMATHES.

BVT I thinke it very strange, that God should permit anie man-kynde (since they beare his owne Image) to fall in so grosse and filthie a defection.

EPI. Although man in his Creation was made to the Image of the Creator[1], yet through his fall having once lost it, it is but restored againe in a part by grace onelie to the elect: So all the rest falling away from God, are given over in the handes of the Devill that enemie, to beare his Image: and being once so given over, the greatest and the grossest impietie, is the pleasantest, and most delytefull vnto them.

PHI. But may it not suffice him to haue indirectly the rule, and procure the perdition of so manie soules by alluring them to vices, and to the following of their own appetites, suppose he abuse not so many simple soules, in making them directlie acknowledge him for their maister.

---

[1] Gen.1.

EPI. No surelie, for hee vses everie man, whom of he hath the rule, according to their complexion and knowledge: And so whome he findes most simple, he plaineliest discovers himselfe vnto them. For hee beeing the enemie of mans Salvation, vses al the meanes he can to entrappe them so farre in his snares, as it may be vnable to them thereafter (suppose they would) to rid themselues out of the same.

PHI. Then this sinne is a sinne against the holie Ghost.

EPI. It is in some, but not in all.

PHI. How that? Are not all these that runnes directlie to the Devill in one Categorie.

EPI. God forbid, for the sin against the holie Ghost hath two branches: The one a falling backe from the whole service of G O D, and a refusall of all his preceptes. The other is the doing of the first with knowledge, knowing that they doe wrong against their own conscience, and the testimonie of the holie Spirit, having once had a tast of the sweetnes of Gods mercies[1]. Now in the first of these two, all sortes of Necromancers, Enchanters or Witches, ar comprehended: but in the last, none but such as erres with this knowledge that I haue spoken of.

PHI Then it appeares that there are more sortes nor one, that are directlie professors of his service: and if so be, I pray you tell me how manie, and what are they?

EPI. There are principallie two sortes, wherevnto all the partes of that vnhappie arte are redacted; whereof the one is called Magie or Necromancie, the other Sorcerie or Witch-craft.

PHI. What I pray you? and how manie are the meanes, whereby the Devill allures persones in anie of these snares?

EPI. Even by these three passiones that are within our selues: Curiositie in great ingines: thrist of revenge, for some tortes

---

[1] Heb. 6

deeply apprehended: or greedie appetite of geare, caused through great pouerty. As to the first of these, Curiosity, it is onelie the inticement of Magiciens, or Necromanciers: and the other two are the allureres of the Sorcerers, or Witches, for that olde and craftie Serpent, being a spirite, hee easilie spyes our affections, and so conformes himselfe thereto, to deceaue vs to our wracke.

# CHAPTER III

## ARGV.

The significations and Etymologies of the words of Magie and Necromancie. The difference betuixt Necromancie and Witch-craft: What are the entressis, and beginninges, that brings anie to the knowledge thereof.

PHILOMATHES.

I Would gladlie first heare, what thing is it that ye call Magie or Necromancie.

EPI. This worde Magie in the Persian toung, importes as muche as to be ane contemplator or Interpretour of Divine and heavenlie sciences: which being first vsed amongs the Chaldees, through their ignorance of the true divinitie, was esteemed and reputed amongst them, as a principall vertue: And therefore, was named vnjustlie with an honorable stile, which name the Greekes imitated, generally importing all these kindes of vnlawfull artes.

And this word Necromancie is a Greek word, compounded of {Greek Nekrwn} & {Greek manteia}, which is to say, the Prophecie by the dead. This last name is given, to this black & vnlawfull science by the figure Synedoche, because it is a principal part of that art, to serue them selues with dead carcages in their diuinations.

PHI. What difference is there betwixt this arte, and Witch-craft.

EPI. Surelie, the difference vulgare put betwixt them, is verrie merrie, and in a maner true; for they say, that the Witches ar servantes onelie, and slaues to the Devil; but the Necromanciers are his maisters and commanders.

PHI. How can that be true, yt any men being specially adicted to his service, can be his co~manders?

EPI. Yea, they may be: but it is onelie secundum quid: For it is not by anie power that they can haue over him, but ex pacto allanerlie: whereby he oblices himself in some trifles to them, that he may on the other part obteine the fruition of their body & soule. which is the onlie thing he huntes for.

PHI. An verie in-æquitable contract forsooth: But I pray you discourse vnto mee, what is the effect and secreets of that arte?

EPI. That is over large an fielde ye giue mee: yet I shall doe good-will, the most summarlie that I can, to runne through the principal points thereof. As there are two sorts of folkes, that may be entysed to this arte, to wit, learned or vnlearned: so is there two meanes, which are the first steerers vp & feeders of their curiositie, thereby to make them to giue themselves over to the same: Which two meanes, I call the Divels schoole, and his rudimentes. The learned haue their curiositie wakened vppe; and fedde by that which I call his schoole: this is the Astrologie judiciar. For divers men having attained to a great perfection in learning, & yet remaining overbare (alas) of the spirit of regeneration and frutes thereof: finding all naturall thinges common, aswell to the stupide pedants as vnto them, they assaie to vendicate vnto them a greater name. by not onlie knowing the course of things heavenlie, but likewise to clim to the knowledge of things to come thereby. Which, at the first face appearing lawfull vnto them, in respect the ground therof seemeth to proceed of naturall causes onelie: they are so allured thereby, that finding their practize to prooue true in sundry things, they studie to know the cause thereof: and so mounting from degree to degree, vpon the slipperie and vncertaine scale of curiositie; they are at last entised, that where lawfull artes or sciences failes, to satisfie their restles mindes, even to seeke to that black and vnlawfull science of Magie. Where, finding at the first. that such diuers formes of circles & conjurations rightlie joyned thereunto, will raise such divers formes of spirites, to resolue them of their doubts: and attributing the doing thereof, to the power inseparablie tyed, or inherent in the circles: and manie words of God, confusedlie wrapped in; they blindlie glorie of themselves, as if they had by their quicknes of ingine, made a conquest of Plutoes dominion, and were become Emperours over the Stygian habitacles. Where, in the meane time (miserable wretches) they are become in verie deede, bond-slaues to their mortall enemie: and their knowledge, for all that they presume thereof, is nothing increased, except in knowing evill, and the horrors of Hell for punishment thereof, as Adams[1] was by the eating of the forbidden tree.

---

[1] Gen. 3

# CHAPTER IIII

## ARGV.

The Description of the Rudiments and Schoole, which are the entresses to the arte of Magie: And in speciall the differences betwixt Astronomie and Astrologie: Diuision of Astrologie in diuers partes.

PHILOMATHES.

BVt I pray you likewise forget not to tell what are the Deuilles rudimentes.

EPI. His rudimentes, I call first in generall, all that which is called vulgarly the vertue of worde, herbe, & stone: which is vsed by vnlawful charmes, without naturall causes. As likewise all kinde of practicques, freites, or other like extraordinarie actiones, which cannot abide the true toutche of naturall reason.

PHI. I would haue you to make that playner, by some particular examples; for your proposition is verie generall.

EPI. I meane either by such kinde of Charmes as commonlie dafte wiues vses, for healing of forspoken goodes, for preseruing them from euill eyes, by knitting roun-trees, or sundriest kinde of herbes, to the haire or tailes of the goodes: By curing the Worme, by stemming of blood, by healing of Horse-crookes, by turning of the riddle, or doing of such like innumerable things by wordes, without applying anie thing, meete to the part offended, as Mediciners doe; Or else by staying maried folkes, to haue naturallie adoe with other, (by knitting so manie knottes vpon a poynt at the time of their mariage) And such-like things, which men vses to practise in their merrinesse: For fra vnlearned men (being naturallie curious, and lacking the true knowledge of God) findes these practises to prooue true, as sundrie of them will doe, by the power of the Devill for deceauing men, and not by anie inherent vertue in these vaine wordes and freites; & being desirous to winne a reputation to themselues in such-like turnes, they either (if they be of the shamefaster sorte) seeke to bee learned by some that are experimented in that Arte, (not knowing it to be euill at the first) or else being of the grosser sorte, runnes directlie to the Deuill for ambition or desire of gaine, and plainelie contractes with him thereupon.

PHI. But me thinkes these meanes which yee call the Schoole and rudimentes of the Deuill, are thinges lawfull, and haue bene approoued for such in all times and ages: As in special, this science of Astrologie, which is one of the speciall members of the Mathematicques.

EPI. There are two thinges which the learned haue obserued from the beginning, in the science of the Heauenlie Creatures, the Planets, Starres, and such like: The one is their course and ordinary motiones, which for that cause is called Astronomia: Which word is a compound of {Greek nomos} & {Greek asterwn} that is to say, the law of the Starres: And this arte indeed is one of the members of the Mathematicques, & not onelie lawful, but most necessarie and commendable. The other is called Astrologia, being compounded of {Greek asterwn} & {Greek logos} which is to say, the word, and preaching of the starres: Which is deuided in two partes: The first by knowing thereby the powers of simples, and sickenesses, the course of the seasons and the weather, being ruled by their influence; which part depending vpon the former, although it be not of it selfe a parte of Mathematicques: yet it is not vnlawful, being moderatlie vsed, suppose not so necessarie and commendable as the former. The second part is to truste so much to their influences, as thereby to fore-tell what commonweales shall florish or decay: what, persones shall be fortunate or vnfortunate: what side shall winne in anie battell: What man shall obteine victorie at singular combate: What way, and of what age shall men die: What horse shall winne at matche-running; and diuerse such like incredible things, wherein Cardanus, Cornelius Agrippa, and diuerse others haue more curiouslie then profitably written at large. Of this roote last spoken of, springs innumerable branches; such as the knowledge by the natiuities; the Cheiromancie, Geomantie, Hydromantie, Arithmantie, Physiognomie: & a thousand others: which were much practised, & holden in great reuerence by the Gentles of olde. And this last part of Astrologie whereof I haue spoken, which is the root of their branches, was called by them pars fortunæ. This parte now is vtterlie vnlawful to be trusted in, or practized amongst christians, as leaning to no ground of natural reason: & it is this part which I called before the deuils schole.

PHI. But yet manie of the learned are of the contrarie opinion.

EPI. I grant, yet I could giue my reasons to fortifie & maintaine my opinion, if to enter into this disputation it wold not draw me quite off the ground of our discours; besides the mis-spending of the whole daie thereupon: One word onely I will answer to them, & that in the Scriptures (which must be an infallible ground to all true Christians) That in the Prophet Ieremie[1] it is plainelie forbidden, to beleeue or hearken vnto them that Prophecies & fore-speakes by the course of the Planets & Starres.

---

[1] Ierem. 10

# CHAPTER V

## ARGV.

How farre the vsing of Charmes is lawfull or vnlawfull: The description of the formes of Circkles and Coniurationes. And what causeth the Magicianes themselues to wearie thereof.

PHILOMATHES.

WELL, Ye haue said far inough in that argument. But how prooue ye now that these charmes or vnnaturall practicques are vnlawfull: For so, many honest & merrie men & women haue publicklie practized some of them, that I thinke if ye would accuse them al of Witch-craft, ye would affirme more nor ye will be beleeued in.

EPI. I see if you had taken good tent (to the nature of that word, whereby I named it,) ye would not haue bene in this doubt, nor mistaken me, so farre as ye haue done: For although, as none can be schollers in a schole, & not be subject to the master thereof: so none can studie and put in practize (for studie the alone, and knowledge, is more perilous nor offensiue; and it is the practise only that makes the greatnes of the offence.) The cirkles and art of Magie, without committing an horrible defection from God: And yet as they that reades and learnes their rudiments, are not the more subject to anie schoole-master, if it please not their parentes to put them to the schoole thereafter; So they who ignorantly proues these practicques, which I cal the deuilles rudiments, vnknowing them to be baites, casten out by him, for trapping such as God will permit to fall in his hands: This kinde of folkes I saie, no doubt, ar to be judged the best of, in respect they vse no invocation nor help of him (by their knowledge at least) in these turnes, and so haue neuer entred themselues in Sathans seruice; Yet to speake truely for my owne part (I speake but for my selfe) I desire not to make so neere riding: For in my opinion our enemie is ouer craftie, and we ouer weake (except the greater grace of God) to assay such hazards, wherein he preases to trap vs.

PHI. Ye haue reason forsooth; for as the common Prouerbe saith: They that suppe keile with the Deuill, haue neede of long spoones. But now I praie you goe forwarde in the describing of this arte of Magie.

EPI. Fra they bee come once vnto this perfection in euill, in hauing any knowledge (whether learned or vnlearned) of this black art: they then beginne to be wearie of the raising of their Maister, by conjured circkles; being both so difficile and perilous, and so commeth plainelie to a contract with him, wherein is speciallie conteined formes and effectes.

PHI. But I praye you or euer you goe further, discourse me somewhat of their circkles and conjurationes; And what should be the cause of their wearying thereof: For it should seeme that that forme should be lesse fearefull yet, than the direct haunting and societie, with that foule and vncleane Spirite.

EPI. I thinke ye take me to be a Witch my selfe, or at the least would faine sweare your selfe prentise to that craft: Alwaies as I may, I shall shortlie satisfie you, in that kinde of conjurations, which are conteined in such bookes, which I call the Deuilles Schoole: There are foure principall partes; the persons of the conjurers; the action of the conjuration; the wordes and rites vsed to that effect; and the Spirites that are conjured. Ye must first remember to laye the ground, that I tould you before: which is, that it is no power inherent in the circles, or in the holines of the names of God blasphemouslie vsed: nor in whatsoeuer rites or ceremonies at that time vsed, that either can raise any infernall spirit, or yet limitat him perforce within or without these circles.

For it is he onelie, the father of all lyes, who hauing first of all prescribed that forme of doing, feining himselfe to he cornmanded & restreined thereby, wil be loath to passe the boundes of these injunctiones; aswell thereby to make them glory in the impiring ouer him (as I saide before:) As likewise to make himselfe so to be trusted in these little thinges, that he may haue the better commoditie thereafter, to deceiue them in the end with a tricke once for all; I meane the euerlasting perdition of their soul & body. Then laying this ground, as I haue said, these conjurationes must haue few or mo in number of the persones conjurers (alwaies passing the singuler number) according to the qualitie of the circle, and forme of apparition. Two principall thinges cannot well in that errand be wanted: holie-water (whereby the Deuill mockes the Papistes) and some present of a liuing thing vnto him. There ar likewise certaine seasons, dayes and houres, that they obserue in this purpose: These things being all readie, and prepared, circles are made triangular, quadrangular, round, double or single, according to the forme of apparition that they craue. But to speake of the diuerse formes of the circles, of the innumerable characters and crosses that are within and without, and out-through the same, of the diuers formes of apparitiones, that that craftie spirit illudes them with, and of all such particulars in that action, I remit it to ouer-manie that haue busied their heades in describing of the same; as being but curious, and altogether vnprofitable. And this farre onelie I touch, that when the conjured Spirit appeares, which will not be while after manie circumstances, long praiers, and much muttring and murmuring of the conjurers; like a Papist priest, dispatching a hunting Masse: how sone I say, he appeares, if they haue missed one iote of all their rites; or if any of their feete once slyd ouer the circle through terror of his fearful apparition, he payes himselfe at that time in his owne hande, of that due debt which they ought him;, and other-wise would haue delayed longer to haue payed him: I meane hee carries them with him bodie and soule. If this be not now a just cause to make them wearie of these formes of conjuration, I leaue it to you to judge vpon; considering the long-somenesse of the labour, the precise keeping of dayes and houres (as I haue said) The terriblenesse of apparition, and the present perrell that they stande in, in missing the least circumstance or freite, that they ought to obserue: And on the other parte, the

Deuil is glad to mooue them to a plaine and square dealing with him as I said before.

# CHAPTER VI

## ARGV.

The Deuilles contract with the Magicians: The diuision thereof in two partes: What is the difference betwixt Gods miracles and the Deuils.

PHILOMATHES.

INdeede there is cause inough, but rather to leaue him at all, then to runne more plainlie to him, if they were wise he delt with. But goe forwarde now I pray you to these turnes, fra they become once deacons in this craft.

EPI. From time that they once plainelie begin to contract with him: The effect of their contract consistes in two thinges; in formes and effectes, as I be gan to tell alreadie, were it not yee interrupted me (for although the contract be mutuall; I speake first of that part, wherein the Deuill oblishes himselfe to them) by formes, I meane in what shape or fashion he shall come vnto them, when they call vpon him. And by effectes, I vnderstand, in what special sorts of seruices he bindes himselfe to be subject vnto them. The qualitie of these formes and effectes, is lesse or greater, according to the skil and art of the Magician. For as to the formes, to some of the baser sorte of them he oblishes him selfe to appeare at their calling vpon him, by such a proper name which he shewes vnto them, either in likenes of a dog, a Catte, an Ape, or such-like other beast; or else to answere by a voyce onlie. The effects are to answere to such demands, as concernes curing of disseases, their own particular menagery: or such other base things as they require of him.

But to the most curious sorte, in the formes he will oblish himselfe, to enter in a dead bodie, and there out of to giue such answers, of the euent of battels, of maters concerning the estate of commonwelths, and such like other great questions: yea, to some he will be a continuall attender, in forme of a Page: He will permit himselfe to be conjured, for the space of so many yeres, ether in a tablet or a ring, or such like thing, which they may easely carrie about with them: He giues them power to sel such wares to others, whereof some will bee dearer, and some better cheape; according to the lying or true speaking of the Spirit that is conjured therein. Not but that in verie deede, all Devils must be lyars; but so they abuse the simplicitie of these wretches, that becomes their schollers, that they make them beleeue, that at the fall of Lucifer, some Spirites fell in the aire, some in the fire, some in the water, some in the lande: In which Elementes they still remaine. Whereupon they build, that such as fell in the fire, or in the aire, are truer then they, who fell in the water or in the land, which is al but meare trattles, & forged be the author of al deceit. For they fel not be weight, as a solide substance, to stick in any one parte: But the principall part of their fal, consisting in qualitie, by the falling from the grace of God wherein they were created, they continued still thereafter, and shal do while the latter daie, in wandring through the worlde, as Gods hang-men, to execute such turnes as he employes them in. And when anie of them are not occupyed in that, returne they must to their prison in hel (as it is plaine in the miracle that CHRIST wrought at Gennezareth[1]) therein at the latter daie to be all enclosed for euer: and as they deceiue their schollers in this, so do they, in imprinting in them the opinion that there are so manie Princes, Dukes, and Kinges amongst them, euerie one commanding fewer or mo Legions, and impyring in diuers artes, and quarters of the earth. For though that I will not denie that there be a forme of ordour amongst the Angels in

---

[1] Mat. 8.

Heauen, and consequentlie, was amongst them before their fall; yet, either that they bruike the same sensine; or that God will permit vs to know by damned Deuils, such heauenlie mysteries of his, which he would not reueale to vs neither by Scripture nor Prophets, I thinke no Christiane will once thinke it. But by the contrarie of all such mysteries, as he hath closed vp with his seale of secrecie; it becommeth vs to be contented with an humble ignorance, they being thinges not necessarie for our saluation. But to returne to the purpose, as these formes, wherein Sathan oblishes himselfe to the greatest of the Magicians, are wounderfull curious; so are the effectes correspondent vnto the same: For he will oblish himselfe to teach them artes and sciences, which he may easelie doe, being so learned a knaue as he is: To carrie them newes from anie parte of the worlde, which the agilitie of a Spirite may easelie performe: to reueale to them the secretes of anie persons, so being they bee once spoken, for the thought none knowes but G O D; except so far as yee may ghesse by their countenance, as one who is doubtleslie learned inough in the Physiognomie: Yea, he will make his schollers to creepe in credite with Princes, by fore-telling them manie greate thinges; parte true, parte false: For if all were false, he would tyne credite at all handes; but alwaies doubtsome, as his Oracles were. And he will also make them to please Princes, by faire banquets and daintie dishes, carryed in short space fra the farthest part of the worlde. For no man doubts but he is a thiefe, and his agilitie (as I spake before) makes him to come suche speede. Such-like, he will guard his schollers with faire armies of horse-men and foote-men in appearance, castles and fortes: Which all are but impressiones in the aire, easelie gathered by a spirite, drawing so neare to that substance himselfe: As in like maner he will learne them manie juglarie trickes at Cardes, dice, & such like, to deceiue mennes senses thereby: and such innumerable false practicques; which are prouen by ouer-manie in this age: As they who ar acquainted with that Italian called SCOTO yet liuing, can reporte. And yet are all these thinges but deluding of the senses, and no waies true in substance, as were the false miracles wrought by King Pharaoes Magicians, for counterfeiting Moyses: For that is the difference betuixt Gods myracles and the Deuils, God is a creator, what he makes appeare in miracle, it is so in effect. As Moyses rod being casten downe, was no doubt turned in a natural Serpent: where as the Deuill (as Gods Ape) counterfetting that by his Magicians, maid their wandes to appeare so, onelie to mennes outward senses: as kythed in effect by their being deuoured by the other. For it is no wonder, that the Deuill may delude our senses, since we see by common proofe, that simple juglars will make an hundreth thinges seeme both to our eies and eares otherwaies then they are. Now as to the Magicians parte of the contract, it is in a word that thing, which I said before, the Deuill hunts for in all men.

PHI. Surelie ye haue said much to me in this arte, if all that ye haue said be as true as wounderfull.

EPI. For the trueth in these actiones, it will be easelie confirmed, to anie that pleases to take paine vpon the reading of diuerse authenticque histories, and the inquiring of daily experiences. And as for the trueth of their possibilitie, that they may be, and in what maner, I trust I haue alleaged nothing whereunto I haue not joyned such probable reasons, as I leaue to your discretion, to waie and consider: One word onlie I omitted; concerning the forme of making of this contract, which is either written with the Magicians owne bloud: or else being agreed vpon (in termes his schole-master) touches him in some parte, though peraduenture no marke remaine: as it doth with all Witches.

# CHAPTER VII

## ARGV.

The reason why the art of Magie is vnlawfull. What punishment they merite: And who may he accounted guiltie of that crime.

PHILOMATHES.

SVRELIE Ye haue made this arte to appeare verie monstruous & detestable. But what I pray you shall be said to such as mainteines this art to be lawfull, for as euill as you haue made it?

EPI. I say, they sauour of the panne them selues, or at least little better, And yet I would be glad to heare their reasons.

PHI. There are two principallie, that euer I heard vsed; beside that which is founded vpon the co~mon Prouerb (that the Necromancers commands the Deuill, which ye haue already refuted) The one is grounded vpon a receiued custome: The other vpon an authoritie, which some thinkes infallible. Vpon custome, we see that diuerse Christian Princes and Magistrates seuere punishers of Witches, will not onelie ouer-see Magicians to liue within their dominions; but euen some-times delight to see them prooue some of their practicques. The other reason is, that Moyses being brought vp (as it is expreslie said in the Scriptures) in all the sciences of the AEgyptians; whereof no doubt, this was one of the principalles. And he notwithstanding of this arte, pleasing God, as he did, consequentlie that art professed by so godlie a man, coulde not be vnlawfull.

EPI. As to the first of your reasones, grounded vpon custome: I saie, an euill custome can neuer be accepted for a good law, for the ouer great ignorance of the worde in some Princes and Magistrates, and the contempt thereof in others, moues them to sinne heavelie against their office in that poynt. As to the other reasone, which seemes to be of greater weight, if it were formed in a Syllogisme; it behooued to be in manie termes, and full of fallacies (to speake in termes of Logicque) for first, that that generall proposition; affirming Moyses to be taught in all the sciences of the AEgyptians, should conclude that he was taught in Magie, I see no necessity. For we must vnderstand that the spirit of God there, speaking of sciences, vnderstandes them that are lawfull; for except they be lawfull, they are but abusiuè called sciences, & are but ignorances indeede: Nam homo pictus, non est homo. Secondlie, giuing that he had bene taught in it, there is great difference, betwixt knowledge and practising of a thing (as I said before) For God knoweth all thinges, being alwaies good, and of our sinne & our infirmitie proceedeth our ignorance. Thirdlie, giuing that he had both studied and practised the same (which is more nor monstruous to be beleeued by any Christian) yet we know well inough, that before that euer the spirite of God began to call Moyses, he was fled out of AEgypt, being fourtie yeares of age, for the slaughter of an AEgyptian, and in his good-father Iethroes lande, first called at the firie bushe, hauing remained there other fourtie yeares in exile: so that suppose he had beene the wickeddest man in the worlde before, he then became a changed and regenerat man, and very litle of olde Moyses remained in him. Abraham was an Idolater in Vr of Chaldæa, before he was called: And Paule being called Saule, was a most sharp persecutor of the Saintes of God, while that name was changed.

PHI. What punishment then thinke ye merites these Magicians and Necromancers?

EPI. The like no doubt, that Sorcerers and Witches merites; and rather so much greater, as their error proceedes of the greater knowledge, and so drawes nerer to the sin against the holy Ghost. And as I saye of them, so saye I the like of all such as consults, enquires, entertaines, & ouersees them, which is seene by the miserable endes of many that askes councell of them: For the Deuill hath neuer better tydings to tell to any, then he tolde to Saule: neither is it lawfull to vse so vnlawfull instrumentes, were it neuer for so good a purpose: for that axiome in Theologie is most certaine and infallible: Nunquam faciendum est malum vt bonum inde eueniat.[1]

---

[1] Ast. 3.

# THE SECONDE BOOKE

OF DÆMONOLOGIE
ARGVMENT.

THE DESCRIPTION OF SORCERIE AN WITCH-CRAFT IN
SPECIALL.

# CHAPTER I

## ARGV.

Proued by the Scripture, that such a thing can be: And the reasones refuted of all such as would call it but an imagination and Melancholicque humor.

PHILOMATHES.

NOW Since yee haue satisfied me nowe so fullie, concerning Magie or Necromancie I will pray you to do the like in Sorcerie or Witchcraft.

EPI. That fielde is likewise verie large: and althought in the mouthes; and pennes of manie, yet fewe knowes the trueth thereof, so wel as they beleeue themselues, as I shall so shortely as I can, make you (God willing) as easelie to perceiue.

PHI. But I pray you before ye goe further, let mee interrupt you here with a shorte digression: which is, that manie can scarcely beleeue that there is such a thing as Witch-craft. Whose reasons I wil shortely alleage vnto you, that ye may satisfie me as well in that, as ye haue done in the rest. For first, whereas the Scripture seemes to prooue Witchcraft to be, by diuerse examples, and speciallie by sundrie of the same, which ye haue alleaged, it is thought by some, that these places speakes of Magicians and Necromancers onlie, & not of Witches. As in special, these wise men of Pharaohs, that counterfeited Moyses miracles, were Magicians say they, & not Witches: As likewise that Pythonisse that Saul consulted with: And so was Simon Magus in the new Testament, as that very stile importes. Secondlie, where ye would oppone the dailie practicque, & confession of so manie, that is thought likewise to be but verie melancholicque imaginations of simple rauing creatures. Thirdly, if Witches had such power of Witching of folkes to death, (as they say they haue) there had bene none left aliue long sence in the world, but they: at the least, no good or godlie person of whatsoeuer estate, coulde haue escaped their deuilrie.

EPI. Your three reasons as I take, ar grounded the first of them negatiuè vpon the Scripture: The second affirmatiuè vpon Physicke: And the thirde vpon the certaine proofe of experience. As to your first, it is most true indeede, that all these wise men of Pharaoh were Magicians of art: As likewise it appeares wel that the Pythonisse, with whom Saul consulted, was of that same profession: & so was Simon Magus. But yee omitted to speake of the Lawe of God, wherein are all Magicians, Diuines, Enchanters, Sorcerers, Witches, & whatsouer of that kinde that consultes with the Deuill, plainelie prohibited, and alike threatned against. And besides that, she who had the Spirite of Python, in the Actes[1], whose Spirite was put to silence by the Apostle, coulde be no other thing but a verie Sorcerer or Witch. if ye admit the vulgare distinction, to be in a maner true, whereof I spake in the beginning of our conference. For that spirit whereby she conquested such gaine to her Master, was not at her raising or commanding, as she pleased to appoynt, but spake by her toung, aswel publicklie, as priuatelie: Whereby she seemed to draw nearer to the sort of Demoniakes or possessed, if that conjunction betwixt them, had not bene of her owne consent: as it appeared by her, not being tormented therewith: And by her conquesting of such gaine to her masters (as I haue alreadie said.) As to your second reason grounded vpon Physick, in attributing their confessiones or apprehensiones, to a naturall melancholicque humour: Anie that pleases Physicallie to consider vpon the naturall humour of melancholie, according to all the Physicians, that euer writ thereupon, they sall finde that that will be ouer

---

[1] Act. 16.

short a cloak to couer their knauery with: For as the humor of Melancholic in the selfe is blacke, heauie and terrene, so are the symptomes thereof, in any persones; that are subject therevnto, leannes, palenes, desire of solitude: and if they come to the highest degree therof, mere folie and Manie: where as by the contrarie, a great number of them that euer haue bene convict or confessors of Witchcraft, as may be presently scene by manie that haue at this time confessed: they are by the contrarie, I say, some of them rich and worldly-wise, some of them fatte or corpulent in their bodies, and most part of them altogether giuen ouer to the pleasures of the flesh, continual haunting of companie, and all kind of merrines, both lawfull and vnlawfull, which are thinges directly contrary to the symptomes of Melancholie, whereof I spake, and further experience daylie proues how loath they are to confesse without torture, which witnesseth their guiltines, where by the contrary, the Melancholicques neuer spares to bewray themselues, by their continuall discourses, feeding therby their humor in that which they thinke no crime. As to your third reason, it scarselie merites an answere. For if the deuill their master were not bridled, as the scriptures teacheth vs, suppose there were no men nor women to be his instrumentes, he could finde waies inough without anie helpe of others to wrack al mankinde: wherevnto he employes his whole study, and goeth about like a roaring Lyon (as PETER saith)[1] to that effect, but the limites of his power were set down before the foundations of the world were laid, which he hath not power in the least jote to transgresse. But beside all this, there is ouer greate a certainty to proue that they are, by the daily experience of the harmes that they do, both to men, and whatsoeuer thing men possesses, whome God will permit them to be the instrumentes, so to trouble or visite, as in my discourse of that arte, yee shall heare clearelie proued.

---

[1] 1. Pet. 5.

# CHAPTER II

## ARGV.

The Etymologie and signification of that word of Sorcerie. The first entresse and prentishippe of them that giues themselues to that craft.

PHILOMATHES.

Come on then I pray you, and returne where ye left.

EPI. This word of Sorcerie is a Latine worde, which is taken from casting of the lot, & therefore he that vseth it, is called Sortiarius à sorte. As to the word of Witchcraft, it is nothing but a proper name giuen in our language. The cause wherefore they were called sortiarij, proceeded of their practicques seeming to come of lot or chance: Such as the turning of the riddle: the knowing of the forme of prayers, or such like tokens: If a person diseased woulde liue or dye. And in generall, that name was giuen them for vsing of such charmes, and freites, as that Crafte teacheth them. Manie poynts of their craft and practicques are common betuixt the Magicians and them: for they serue both one Master, althought in diuerse fashions. And as I deuided the Necromancers, into two sorts, learned and vnlearned; so must I denie them in other two, riche and of better accompt, poore and of basser degree. These two degrees now of persones, that practises this craft, answers to the passions in them, which (I told you before) the Deuil vsed as meanes to intyse them to his seruice, for such of them as are in great miserie and pouertie, he allures to follow him, by promising vnto them greate riches, and worldlie commoditie. Such as though riche, yet burnes in a desperat desire of reuenge, hee allures them by promises, to get their turne satisfied to their hartes contentment. It is to be noted nowe, that that olde and craftie enemie of ours, assailes none, though touched with any of these two extremities, except he first finde an entresse reddy for him, either by the great ignorance of the person he deales with, ioyned with an euill life, or else by their carelesnes and contempt of God: And finding them in an vtter despair, for one of these two former causes that I haue spoken of; he prepares the way by feeding them craftely in their humour, and filling them further and further with despaire, while he finde the time proper to discouer himself vnto them. At which time, either vpon their walking solitarie in the fieldes, or else lying pansing in their bed; but alwaies without the company of any other, he either by a voyce, or in likenesse of a man inquires of them, what troubles them: and promiseth them, a suddaine and certaine waie of remedie, vpon condition on the other parte, that they follow his advise; and do such thinges as he wil require of them: Their mindes being prepared before hand, as I haue alreadie spoken, they easelie agreed vnto that demande of his: And syne settes an other tryist, where they may meete againe. At which time, before he proceede any further with them, he first perswades them to addict themselues to his seruice: which being easely obteined, he then discouers what he is vnto them: makes them to renunce their God and Baptisme directlie, and giues them his marke vpon some secreit place of their bodie, which remaines soare vnhealed, while his next meeting with them, and thereafter euer insensible, how soeuer it be nipped or pricked by any, as is dailie proued, to giue them a proofe thereby, that as in that doing, hee could hurte and heale them; so all their ill and well doing thereafter, must depende vpon him. And besides that, the intollerable dolour that they feele in that place, where he hath marked them, serues to waken them, and not to let them rest, while their next meeting againe: fearing least otherwaies they might either forget him, being as new Prentises, and not well inough founded yet, in that fiendlie follie: or else remembring of that horrible promise they made him, at their last meeting, they might skunner at the same, and preasse to call it back. At their thirde meeting, he makes a shew to be carefull, to performe his promises, either by teaching them waies howe to get themselues reuenged, if they be of that sort: Or els by teaching them lessons, how by moste vilde and vnlawfull meanes, they may obtaine gaine, and worldlie commoditie, if they be of the other sorte.

# CHAPTER III

### ARGV.

The Witches actiones diuided in two partes. The actiones proper to their owne persones. Their actiones toward others. The forme of their conuentiones, and adoring of their Master.

PHILOMATHES.

YE haue said now inough of their initiating in that ordour. It restes then that ye discourse vpon their practises, fra they be passed Prentises: for I would faine heare what is possible to them to performe in verie deede. Although they serue a common Master with the Necromancers, (as I haue before saide) yet serue they him in an other forme. For as the meanes are diuerse, which allures them to these vnlawfull artes of seruing of the Deuill; so by diuerse waies vse they their practises, answering to these meanes, which first the Deuill, vsed as instrumentes in them; though al tending to one end: To wit. the enlargeing of Sathans tyrannie, and crossing of the propagation of the Kingdome of CHRIST, so farre as lyeth in the possibilitie, either of the one or other sorte, or of the Deuill their Master. For where the Magicians, as allured by curiositie, in the most parte of their practises, seekes principallie the satisfying of the same, and to winne to themselues a popular honoure and estimation: These Witches on the other parte, being intised ether for the desire of reuenge, or of worldly riches, their whole practises are either to hurte men and their gudes, or what they possesse, for satisfying of their cruell mindes in the former, or else by the wracke in quhatsoeuer sorte, of anie whome God will permitte them to haue power off, to satisfie their greedie desire in the last poynt.

EPI. In two partes their actiones may be diuided; the actiones of their owne persones, and the actiones proceeding from them towardes anie other. And this diuision being wel vnderstood, will easilie resolue you, what is possible to them to doe. For although all that they confesse is no lie vpon their parte, yet doubtlesly in my opinion, a part of it is not indeede, according as they take it to be: And in this I meane by the actiones of their owne persones. For as I said before, speaking of Magie that the Deuill illudes the senses of these schollers of his, in manie thinges, so saye I the like of these Witches.

PHI. Then I pray you, first to speake of that part of their owne persons, and syne ye may come next to their actiones towardes; others.

EPI. To the effect that they may performe such seruices of their false Master, as he employes them in, the deuill as Gods Ape, counterfeites in his seruantes this seruice & forme of adoration, that God prescribed and made his seruantes to practise. For as the seruants of G O D, publicklie vses to conveene for seruing of him, so makes he them in great numbers to conveene (though publickly they dare not) for his seruice. As none conueenes to the adoration and worshipping of God, except they be marked with his seale, the Sacrament of Baptisme: So none serues Sathan, and conueenes to the adoring of him, that are not marked with that marke, wherof I alredy spake. As the Minister sent by God, teacheth plainely at the time of their publick conuentions, how to serue him in spirit & truth: so that vncleane spirite, in his owne person teacheth his Disciples, at the time of their conueening, how to worke all kinde of mischiefe: And craues compt of all their horrible and detestable proceedinges passed, for aduancement of his seruice. Yea, that he may the more viuelie counterfeit and scorne God, he oft times makes his slaues to conveene in these verrie places, which are destinat and ordeined for the conveening of the servantes of God (I meane by Churches) But this farre, which I haue yet said, I not onelie take it to be true in their opiniones, but euen so to be indeede. For the forme that he vsed in counterfeiting God amongst the Gentiles, makes me so to thinke: As God spake by his Oracles, spake he not so by his? As G O D had aswell bloudie Sacrifices, as others without bloud, had not he the like? As God had Churches sanctified to his seruice, with Altars, Priests, Sacrifices, Ceremonies and Prayers; had he not the like polluted to his seruice? As God gaue responses by Vrim and Thummim, gaue he not his responses by the intralls of beastes, by the singing of Fowles, and by their actiones in the aire? As God by visiones, dreames, and extases reueiled what was to come, and what was his will vnto his scruantes; vsed he not the like meanes to forwarne his slaues of things to come? Yea, euen as God loued cleannes, hated vice, and impuritie, & appoynted punishmentes therefore: vsed he not the like (though falselie I grant, and but in eschewing the lesse inconuenient, to draw them upon a greater) yet dissimuled he not I say, so farre as to appoynt his Priestes to keepe their bodies cleane and vndefiled, before their asking responses of him? And feyned he not God to be a protectour of euerie vertue, and a iust reuenger of the contrarie? This reason then moues me. that as he is that same Deuill; and as craftie nowe as he was then; so wil hee not spare a pertelie in these actiones that I haue spoken of, concerning the witches persones: But further, Witches oft times confesses not only his conueening in the Church with them, but his occupying of the Pulpit: Yea, their forme of adoration, to be the kissing of his hinder partes. Which though it seeme ridiculous, yet may it likewise be true, seeing we reade that in Calicute, he appearing in forme of a Goate-bucke, hath publicklie that vn-honest homage done vnto him, by euerie one of the people: So ambitious is he, and greedie of honour (which procured his fall) that he will euen imitate God in that parte, where it is said, that Moyses could see but the hinder partes of God, for the brightnesse of his glorie:[1] And yet that speache is spoken but {Greek anðrwpwpaðeian}

---

[1] Exo. 33

# CHAPTER IIII

## ARGV.

What are the waies possible, wherby the witches may transport themselues to places far distant. And what ar impossible &mere illusiones of Sathan. And the reasons therof.

PHILOMATHES.

Bvt by what way say they or think ye it possible that they can com to these vnlawful co~uentio~s?

EPI. There is the thing which I esteeme their senses to be deluded in, and though they lye not in confessing of it, because they thinke it to be true, yet not to be so in substance or effect: for they saie, that by diuerse meanes they may conueene, either to the adoring of their Master, or to the putting in practise any seruice of his, committed vnto their charge: one way is natural, which is natural riding, going or sayling, at what houre their Master comes and aduertises them. And this way may be easelie beleued: an other way is some-what more strange: and yet is it possible to be true: which is by being carryed by the force of the Spirite which is their conducter, either aboue the earth or aboue the Sea swiftlie, to the place where they are to meet: which I am perswaded to be likewaies possible, in respect that as Habakkuk was carryed by the Angell in that forme, to the denne where Daniell laie;[1] so thinke I,

---

[1] Apocrypha of Bell and the Dragon.

the Deuill will be reddie to imitate God, as well in that as in other thinges: which is much more possible to him to doe, being a Spirite, then to a mighty winde, being but a naturall meteore, to transporte from one place to an other a solide bodie, as is commonlie and dailie seene in practise: But in this violent forme they cannot be carryed, but a shorte boundes, agreeing with the space that they may reteine their breath: for if it were longer, their breath could not remaine vnextinguished, their bodie being carryed in such a violent & forceable maner, as be example: If one fall off an small height, his life is but in perrell, according to the harde or soft lighting: But if one fall from an high and stay rocke, his breath wilbe forceablie banished from the bodie, before he can win to the earth, as is oft seen by experience. And in this transporting they say themselues, that they are inuisible to anie other, except amongst themselues; which may also be possible in my opinion. For if the deuil may forme what kinde of impressiones he pleases in the aire, as I haue said before, speaking of Magie, why may he not far easilier thicken & obscure so the air, that is next about them by contracting it strait together, that the beames of any other mans eyes, cannot pearce thorow the same, to see them? But the third way of their comming to their conuentions, is, that where in I think them deluded: for some of them sayeth, that being transformed in the likenesse of a little beast or foule, they will come and pearce through whatsoeuer house or Church, though all ordinarie passages be closed, by whatsoeuer open, the aire may enter in at. And some sayeth, that their bodies lying stil as in an extasy, their spirits wil be rauished out of their bodies, & caried to such places. And for verefying therof, wil giue euident tokens, aswel by witnesses that haue seene their body lying senseless in the meane time, as by naming persones, whomwith they mette, and giuing tokens quhat purpose was amongst them, whome otherwaies they could not haue knowen: for this forme of journeing, they affirme to vse most, when they are transported from one Countrie to another.

PHI. Surelie I long to heare your owne opinion of this: For they are like old wiues trattles about the fire. The reasons that moues me to thinke that these are meere illusiones, ar these. First for them that are transformed in likenes of beastes or foules, can enter through so narrow passages, although I may easelie beleeue that the Deuill coulde by his woorkemanshippe vpon the aire, make them appeare to be in such formes, either to themselues or to others: Yet how he can contract a solide bodie within so little roome, I thinke it is directlie contrarie to it selfe, for to be made so little, and yet not diminished: To be so straitlie drawen together, and yet feele no paine; I thinke it is so contrarie to the qualitie of a naturall bodie, and so like to the little transubstantiat god in the Papistes Masse, that I can neuer beleeue it. So to haue a quantitie, is so proper to a solide bodie, that as all Philosophers concludes, it cannot be any more without one, then a spirite can haue one. For when PETER came out of the prison, and the doores all locked:[1] It was not by any contracting of his bodie in so little roome: but by the giuing place of the dore, though vn-espyed by the Gaylors. And yet is there no comparison, when this is done, betuixt the power of God, and of the Deuill. As to their forme of extasie and spirituall transporting, it is certaine the soules going out of the bodie, is the onely difinition of naturall death: and who are once dead, God forbid wee should thinke that it should lie in the power of all the Deuils in Hell, to restore them to their life againe: Although he can put his owne spirite in a dead bodie, which the Necromancers commonlie practise, as yee haue harde. For that is the office properly belonging to God; and besides that, the soule once parting from the bodie, cannot wander anie longer in the worlde, but to the owne resting place must it goe immediatlie, abiding the conjunction of the bodie againe, at the latter daie. And what CHRIST or the Prophets did miraculouslie in this case, it cannot in no Christian mans opinion be maid common with the Deuill. As for anie tokens that they giue for proouing of this, it is verie possible to the Deuils craft, to perswade them to these meanes. For he being a spirite, may hee: not so rauishe their thoughtes, and dull their sences, that their bodie lying as dead, hee may object to their spirites as it were in a dreame, & (as the Poets write of Morpheus) represente such formes of persones, of places, and other circumstances, as he pleases to illude them with? Yea, that he maie deceiue them with the greater efficacie, may hee not at that same instant, by fellow angelles of his, illude such other persones so in that same fashion, whome with he makes them to beleeue that they mette; that all their reportes and tokens, though seuerallie examined, may euerie one agree with an other. And that whatsoeuer actiones, either in

---

[1] Act. 12.

hurting men or beasts: or whatsoeuer other thing that they falselie imagine, at that time to haue done, may by himselfe or his marrowes, at that same time be done indeede; so as if they would giue for a token of their being rauished at the death of such a person within so shorte space thereafter, whom they beleeue to haue poysoned, or witched at that instante, might hee not at that same houre, haue smitten that same person by the permission of G O D, to the farther deceiuing of them, and to mooue others to beleeue them? And this is surelie the likeliest way, and most according to reason, which my judgement can finde out in this, and whatsoeuer vther vnnaturall poyntes of their confession. And by these meanes shall we saill surelie, betuixt Charybdis and Scylla, in eschewing the not beleeuing of them altogether on the one part, least that drawe vs to the errour that there is no Witches: and on the other parte in beleeuing of it, make vs to eschew the falling into innumerable absurdities, both monstruouslie against all Theologie diuine, and Philosophie humaine.

# CHAPTER V

## ARGV.

Witches actiones towardes others. Why there are more women of that craft nor men? What thinges are possible to them to effectuate by the power of their master. The reasons thereof. What is the surest remedie of the harmes done by them.

PHILOMATHES.

Forsooth your opinion in this, seemes to carrie most reason with it, and sence yee haue ended, then the actions belonging properly to their owne persones: say forwarde now to their actiones vsed towardes others.

EPI. In their actiones vsed towardes others, three thinges ought to be considered: First the maner of their consulting thereupon: Next their part as instrumentes: And last their masters parte, who puts the same in execution. As to their consultationes thereupon, they vse them oftest in the Churches, where they conveene for adoring: at what time their master enquiring at them what they would be at: euerie one of them propones vnto him, what wicked turne they would haue done, either for obteining of riches, or for reuenging them vpon anie whome they haue malice at: who granting their demande, as no doubt willinglie he wil, since it is to doe euill, he teacheth them the means, wherby they may do the same. As for little trifling turnes that women haue ado with, he causeth them to ioynt dead corpses, & to make powders thereof, mixing such other thinges there amongst, as he giues vnto them.

PHI. But before yee goe further, permit mee I pray you to interrupt you one worde, which yee haue put mee in memorie of, by speaking of Women. What can be the cause that there are twentie women giuen to that craft, where ther is one man?

EPI. The reason is easie, for as that sexe is frailer then man is, so is it easier to be intrapped in these grosse snares of the Deuill, as was ouer well proued to be true, by the Serpents deceiuing of Eua at the beginning, which makes him the homelier with that sexe sensine.

PHI. Returne now where ye left.

EPI. To some others at these times hee teacheth, how to make Pictures of waxe or clay: That by the rosting thereof, the persones; that they beare the name of, may be continuallie melted or dryed awaie by continuall sicknesse. To some hee giues such stones or poulders, as will helpe to cure or cast on diseases: And to some he teacheth kindes of vncouthe poysons, which Mediciners vnderstandes not (for he is farre cunningner then man in the knowledge of all the occult proprieties of nature) not that anie of these meanes which hee teacheth them (except the poysons which are composed of thinges naturall) can of them selues helpe any thing to these turnes, that they are employed in, but onelie being Gods Ape, as well in that, as in all other thinges. Even as God by his Sacramentes which are earthlie of themselues workes a heavenlie effect, though no waies by any cooperation in them: And as CHRIST by clay & spettle wrought together, opened the eies of the blynd man,[1] suppose there was no vertue in that which he outwardlie applyed, so the Deuill will haue his out-warde meanes to be shewes as it were of his doing, which hath no part of cooperation in his turnes with him, how farre that euer the ignorantes be abused in the contrarie. And as to the effectes of these two former partes, to wit, the consultationes and the outward meanes, they are so wounderfull as I dare not allege anie of them, without ioyning a sufficient reason of the possibilitie

---

[1] John. 9.

thereof. For leauing all the small trifles among wiues, and to speake of the principall poyntes of their craft. For the common trifles thereof, they can do without conuerting well inough by themselues: These principall poyntes I say are these: They can make men or women to loue or hate other, which may be verie possible to the Deuil to effectuat, seing he being a subtile spirite, knowes well inough how to perswade the corrupted affection of them whom God will permit him so to deale with: They can lay the siknesse of one vpon an other, which likewise is verie possible vnto him: For since by Gods permission, he layed siknesse vpon IOB, why may he not farre easilier lay it vpon any other: For as an old practisian, he knowes well inough what humor domines most in anie of vs, and as a spirite hee can subtillie walken vp the same, making it peccant, or to abounde, as he thinkes meete for troubling of vs, when God will so permit him. And for the taking off of it, no doubt he will be glad to reliue such of present paine, as he may thinke by these meanes to perswade to bee catched in his euerlasting snares and fetters. They can be-witch and take the life of men or women, by rosting of the Pictures, as I spake of before, which likewise is verie possible to their Master to performe, for although, (as I saide before) that instrumente of waxe haue no vertue in that turne doing, yet may hee not verie well euen by that same measure that his conjured slaues meltes that waxe at the fire, may he not I say at these same times, subtilie as a spirite so weaken and scatter the spirites of life of the patient, as may make him on th'one part, for faintnesse to sweate out the humour of his bodie: And on the other parte, for the not concurrence of these spirites, which causes his digestion, so debilitat his stomak, that his humour radicall continually, sweating out on the one parte, and no new good suck being put in the place thereof, for lack of digestion on the other, hee at last shall vanish awaie, euen as his picture will doe at the fire. And that knauish and cunning woorkeman, by troubling him onely at some times, makes a proportion so neare betuixt the woorking of the one and the other, that both shall ende as it were at one time. They can rayse stormes and tempestes in the aire, either vpon Sea or land, though not vniuersally, but in such a particular place and prescribed boundes, as God will permitte them so to trouble: Which likewise is verie easie to be discerned from anie other naturall tempestes that are meteores, in respect of the suddaine and violent raising thereof, together with the short induring of the same. And this is likewise verie possible to their master to do, he hauing such affinitie with the aire as being a spirite, and hauing such power of the forming and moouing thereof, as ye haue heard me alreadie declare: For in the Scripture, that stile of the Prince of the aire is giuen vnto him[1]. They can make folkes to becom phrenticque or Maniacque, which likewise is very possible to their master to do, sence they are but naturall sicknesses: and so he may lay on these kindes, aswell as anie others. They can make spirites either to follow and trouble persones, or haunt certaine houses. and affraie oftentimes the inhabitantes: as hath bene knowen to be done by our Witches at this time. And likewise they can make some to be possessed with spirites, & so to becom verie Dæmoniacques: and this last sorte is verie possible likewise to the Deuill their Master to do, since he may easilie send his owne angells to trouble in what forme he pleases, any whom God wil permit him so to vse.

PHI. But will God permit these wicked instrumentes by the power of the Deuill their master, to trouble by anie of these meanes, anie that beleeues in him?

EPI. No doubt, for there are three kinde of folkes whom God will permit so to be tempted or troubled; the wicked for their horrible sinnes, to punish them in the like measure; The godlie that are sleeping in anie great sinnes or infirmities and weakenesse in faith, to waken them vp the faster by such an vncouth forme: and euen some of the best, that their patience may bee tryed before the world, as IOBs was. For why may not God vse anie kinde of extraordinarie punishment, when it pleases him; as well as the ordinarie roddes of sicknesse or other aduersities.

PHI. Who then may he free from these Deuilish practises?

EPI. No man ought to presume so far as to promise anie impunitie to himselfe: for God hath before all beginninges preordinated aswell the particular sortes of Plagues as of benefites for euerie man, which in the owne time he ordaines them to be visited with, & yet ought we not to be the more affrayde for that, of any thing that the Deuill and his wicked instrumentes can do against vs..

---

[1] Ephes. 2.

For we dailie fight against the Deuill in a hundreth other waies: And therefore as a valiant Captaine, affraies no more being at the combat, nor stayes from his purpose for the rummishing shot of a Cannon, nor the small clack of a Pistoler: suppose he be not certaine what may light vpon him; Euen so ought we boldlie to goe forwarde in fighting against the Deuill without anie greater terrour, for these his rarest weapons, nor for the ordinarie whereof wee haue daily the proofe.

PHI. Is it not lawfull then by the helpe of some other Witche to cure the disease that is casten on by that craft?

EPI. No waies lawfull: For I gaue you the reason thereof in that axiome of Theologie, which was the last wordes I spake of Magie

PHI. How then may these diseases he lawfullie cured?

EPI. Onelie by earnest prayer to G O D, by amendement of their liues, and by sharp persewing euerie one, according to his calling of these instrumentes of Sathan, whose punishment to the death will be a salutarie sacrifice for the patient. And this is not onely the lawfull way, but likewise the most sure: For by the Deuils meanes, can neuer the Deuill be casten out,[1] as Christ sayeth. And when such a cure is vsed, it may wel serue for a shorte time, but at the Last, it will doubtleslie tend to the vtter perdition of the patient, both in bodie and soule.

---

[1] Math. 3

# CHAPTER VI

## ARGV.

What sorte of folkes are least or most subiect to receiue harme by Witchcraft. What power they haue to harme the Magistrate, and vpon what respectes they haue any power in prison: And to what end may or will the Deuill appeare to them therein. Vpon what respectes the Deuill appeires in sundry shapes to sundry of them at any time.

PHILOMATHES. BVt who dare take vpon him to punish them, if no man can be sure to be free from their vnnaturall inuasiones?

EPI. We ought not the more of that restraine from vertue, that the way wherby we climbe thereunto be straight and perrilous. But besides that, as there is no kinde of persones so subject to receiue harme of them, as these that are of infirme and weake faith (which is the best buckler against such inuasiones:) so haue they so smal power ouer none) as ouer such as zealouslie and earnestlie persewes them, without sparing for anie worldlie respect.

PHI. Then they are like the Pest, which smites these sickarest, that flies it farthest, and apprehends deepliest the perrell thereof.

EPI. It is euen so with them: For neither is it able to them to vse anie false cure vpon a patient, except the patient first beleeue in their power, and so hazard the tinsell of his owne soule, nor yet can they haue lesse power to hurte anie, nor such as contemnes most their doinges, so being it comes of faith, and not of anie vaine arrogancie in themselues.

PHI. But what is their power against the Magistrate?

EPI. Lesse or greater, according as he deales with them. For if he be slouthfull towardes them, God is verie able to make them instrumentes to waken & punish his slouth. But if he be the contrarie, he according to the iust law of God, and allowable law of all Nationes, will be diligent in examining and punishing of them: G O D will not permit their master to trouble or hinder so good a woorke.

PHI. But fra they be once in handes and firmance, haue they anie further power in their craft?

EPI. That is according to the forme of their detention. If they be but apprehended and deteined by anie priuate person, vpon other priuate respectes, their power no doubt either in escaping, or in doing hurte, is no lesse nor euer it was before. But if on the other parte, their apprehending and detention be by the lawfull Magistrate, vpon the iust respectes of their guiltinesse in that craft, their power is then no greater then before that euer they medled with their master. For where God beginnes iustlie to strike by his lawfull Lieutennentes, it is not in the Deuilles power to defraude or bereaue him of the office, or effect of his powerfull and reuenging Scepter.

PHI. But will neuer their master come to visite them, fra they be once apprehended and put in firmance?

EPI. That is according to the estaite that these miserable wretches are in: For if they be obstinate in still denying, he will not spare, when he findes time to speake with them, either if he finde them in anie comfort, to fill them more and more with the vaine hope of some maner of reliefe: or else if hee finde them in a deepe dispaire, by all meanes to augment the same, and to perswade them by some extraordinarie meanes to put themselues downe, which verie commonlie they doe. But if they be penitent and confesse, God will not permit him to trouble them anie more with his presence and alurementes.

PHI It is not good vsing his counsell I see then. But I woulde earnestlie know when he appeares to them in Prison, what formes vses he then to take?

EPI. Diuers formes, euen as he vses to do at other times vnto them. For as I told you, speking of Magie, lie appeares to that kinde of craftes-men ordinarily in an forme, according as they agree vpon it amongst themselues: Or if they be but prentises, according to the qualitie of their circles or conjurationes: Yet to these capped creatures, he appeares as he pleases, and as he findes meetest for their humors. For euen at their publick conuentiones, he appeares to diuers of them in diuers formes, as we haue found by the difference of their confessiones in that point: For he deluding them with vaine impressiones in the aire, makes himselfe to seeme more terrible to the grosser sorte, that they maie thereby be moued to feare and reuerence him the more: And les monstrous and vncouthlike againe to the craftier sorte, least otherwaies they might sturre and skunner at his vglinesse.

PHI. How can he then be felt. as they confesse they haue done him, if his bodie be but of aire?

EPI. I heare little of that amongst their confessiones, yet may he make himselfe palpable, either by assuming any dead bodie, and vsing the ministrie thereof, or else by deluding as wel their sence of feeling as seeing; which is not impossible to him to doe, since all our senses, as we are so weake, and euen by ordinarie sicknesses will be often times deluded.

PHI. But I would speere one worde further yet, concerning his appearing to them in prison, which is this. May any other that chances to be present at that time in the prison, see him as well as they.

EPI. Some-times they will, and some-times not, as it pleases God.

# CHAPTER VII

### ARGV.

Two formes of the deuils visible conuersing in the earth, with the reasones wherefore the one of them was communest in the time of Papistrie: And the other sensine. Those that denies the power of the Deuill, denies the power of God, and are guiltie of the errour of the Sadduces.

PHILOMATHES.

HAth the Deuill then power to appeare to any other, except to such as are his sworne disciples: especially since al Oracles, & such like kinds of illusiones were taken awaie and abolished by the cumming Of CHRIST?

EPI. Although it be true indeede, that the brightnesse of the Gospell at his cumming, scaled the cloudes of all these grosse errors in the Gentilisme: yet that these abusing spirites, ceases not sensine at sometimes to appeare, dailie experience teaches vs. Indeede this difference is to be marked betwixt the formes of Sathans conuersing visiblie in the world. For of two different formes thereof, the one of them by the spreading of the Euangell, and conquest of the white horse, in the sixt Chapter of the Reuelation, is much hindred and become rarer there through. This his appearing to any Christians, troubling of them outwardly, or possessing of them constraynedly. The other of them is be-

become communer and more vsed sensine, I meane by their vnlawfull artes, whereupon our whole purpose hath bene. This we finde by experience in this Ile to be true. For as we know, moe Ghostes and spirites were seene, nor tongue can tell, in the time of blinde Papistrie in these Countries, where now by the contrarie, a man shall scarcely all his time here once of such things. And yet were these vnlawfull artes farre rarer at that time: and neuer were so much harde of, nor so rife as they are now.

PHI. What should be the cause of that?

EPI. The diuerse nature of our sinnes procures at the Iustice of God, diuerse sortes of punishments answering thereunto. And therefore as in the time of Papistrie, our fathers erring grosselie, & through ignorance, that mist of errours ouershaddowed the Deuill to walke the more familiarlie amongst them: And as it were by barnelie and affraying terroures, to mocke and accuse their barnelie erroures. By the contrarie, we now being sounde of Religion, and in our life rebelling to our profession, God iustlie by that sinne of rebellion, as Samuel calleth it, accuseth our life so wilfullie fighting against our profession.

PHI. Since yee are entred now to speake of the appearing of spirites: I would be glad to heare your opinion in that matter. For manie denies that anie such spirites can appeare in these daies as I haue said.

EPI. Doubtleslie who denyeth the power of the Deuill, woulde likewise denie the power of God, if they could for shame. For since the Deuill is the verie contrarie opposite to God, there can be no better way to know God, then by the contrarie; as by the ones power (though a creature) to admire the power of the great Creator: by the falshood of the one to consider the trueth of the other, by the injustice of the one, to considder the Iustice of the other: And by the cruelty of the one, to considder the mercifulnesse of the other: And so foorth in all the rest of the essence of God, and qualities of the Deuill. But I feare indeede, there be ouer many Sadduces in this worlde, that denies all kindes of spirites: For convicting of whose errour, there is cause inough if there were no more, that God should permit at sometimes spirits visiblie to kyith.

# THE THIRDE BOOKE

### OF DÆMONOLOGIE
### ARGVMENT

THE DESCRIPTION OF ALL THESE KINDES OF SPIRITES THAT TROUBLES MEN OR WOMEN. THE CONCLUSION OF THE WHOLE DIALOGUE.

# CHAPTER I

### ARGV.

The diuision of spirites in foure principall kindes. The description of the first kinde of them, called Spectra & vmbræ mortuorum. What is the best way to be free of their trouble.

PHILOMATHES.

I Pray you now then go forward in telling what ye thinke fabulous, or may be trowed in that case.

EPI. That kinde of the Deuils conuersing in the earth, may be diuided in foure different kindes, whereby he affrayeth and troubleth the bodies of men: For of the abusing of the soule, I haue spoken alreadie. The first is, where spirites troubles some houses or solitarie places: The second, where spirites followes vpon certaine persones, and at diuers houres troubles them: The thirde, when they enter within them and possesse them: The fourth is these kinde of spirites that are called vulgarlie the Fayrie. Of the three former kindes, ye harde alreadie, how they may artificiallie be made by Witch-craft to trouble folke: Now it restes to speake of their naturall comming as it were, and not raysed by Witch-craft. But generally I must for-warne you of one thing before I enter in this purpose: that is, that although in my discourseing of them, I deuyde them in diuers kindes, yee must notwithstanding there of note my Phrase of speaking in that: For doubtleslie they are in effect, but all one kinde of spirites, who for abusing the more of mankinde. takes on these sundrie shapes, and vses diuerse formes of out-ward actiones, as if some were of nature better then other. Nowe I returne to my purpose: As to the first kinde of these spirites, that were called by the auncients by diuers names, according as their actions were. For if they were spirites that haunted some houses, by appearing in diuers and horrible formes, and making greate dinne: they were called Lemures or Spectra. If they appeared in likenesse of anie defunct to some friends of his, they wer called vmbræ mortuorum: And so innumerable stiles they got, according to their actiones, as I haue said alreadie. As we see by experience, how manie stiles they haue given them in our language in the like maner: Of the appearing of these spirites, wee are certified by the Scriptures, where the Prophet ESAY 13. and 34. cap. threatning the destruction of Babell and Edom:[1] declares, that it shal not onlie be wracked, but shall become so greate a solitude, as it shall be the habitackle of Howlettes, and of ZIIM and IIM, which are the proper Hebrewe names for these Spirites. The cause whie they haunte solitarie places, it is by reason, that they may affraie and brangle the more the faith of suche as them alone hauntes such places. For our nature is such, as in companies wee are not so soone mooued to anie such kinde of feare, as being solitare, which the Deuill knowing well inough, hee will not therefore assaile vs but when we are weake: And besides that, G O D will not permit him so to dishonour the societies and companies of Christians, as in publicke times and places to walke visiblie amongst them. On the other parte, when he troubles certaine houses that are dwelt in, it is a sure token either of grosse ignorance, or of some grosse and slanderous sinnes amongst the inhabitantes thereof: which God by that extraordinarie rod punishes.

PHI. But by what way or passage can these Spirites enter in these houses, seeing they alledge that they will enter, Doore and Window being steiked?

EPI. They will choose the passage for their entresse, according to the forme that they are in at that time. For if they haue assumed a deade bodie, whereinto they lodge themselues, they can easely

---

[1] Esay. 13 Iere. 50

inough open without dinne anie Doore or Window, and enter in thereat. And if they enter as a spirite onelie, anie place where the aire may come in at, is large inough an entrie for them: For as I said before, a spirite can occupie no quantitie.

PHI. And will God then permit these wicked spirites to trouble the reste of a dead bodie, before the resurrection thereof? Or if he will so, I thinke it should be of the reprobate onely.

EPI. What more is the reste troubled of a dead bodie, when the Deuill carryes it out of the Graue to serue his turne for a space, nor when the Witches takes it vp and joyntes it, or when as Swine wortes vppe the graues? The rest of them that the Scripture speakes of, is not meaned by a locall remaining continuallie in one place, but by their resting from their trauelles and miseries of this worlde, while their latter conjunction againe with the soule at that time to receaue full glorie in both. And that the Deuill may vse aswell the ministrie of the bodies of the faithfull in these cases, as of the vn-faithfull, there is no inconvenient; for his haunting with their bodies after they are deade, can no-waies defyle them: In respect of the soules absence. And for anie dishonour it can be vnto them, by what reason can it be greater, then the hanging, heading, or many such shameful deaths, that good men will suffer? for there is nothing in the bodies of the faithfull, more worthie of honour, or freer from corruption by nature, nor in these of the vnfaithful, while time they be purged and glorified in the latter daie, as is dailie seene by the vilde diseases and corruptions, that the bodies of the faythfull are subject vnto, as yee will see clearelie proued, when I speake of the possessed and Dæmoniacques.

PHI. Yet there are sundrie that affirmes to haue haunted such places, where these spirites are alleaged to be: And coulde neuer heare nor see anie thing.

EPI. I thinke well: For that is onelie reserued to the secreete knowledge of God, whom he wil permit to see such thinges, and whome not.

PHI. But where these spirites hauntes and troubles anie houses, what is the best waie to banishe them?

EPI. By two meanes may onelie the remeid of such things be procured: The one is ardent prayer to God, both of these persones that are troubled with them, and of that Church whereof they are. The other is the purging of themselues by amende ment of life from such sinnes. as haue procured that extraordinarie plague.

PHI. And what meanes then these kindes of spirites, when they appeare in the shaddow of a person newlie dead, or to die, to his friendes?

EPI. When they appeare vpon that occasion, they are called Wraithes in our language. Amongst the Gentiles the Deuill vsed that much, to make them beleeue that it was some good spirite that appeared to them then, ether to forewarne them of the death of their friend; or else to discouer vnto them, the will of the defunct, or what was the way of his slauchter, as is written in the booke of the histories Prodigious. And this way hee easelie decciued the Gentiles, because they knew not God: And to that same effect is it, that he now appeares in that maner to some ignorant Christians. For he dare not so illude anie that knoweth that, neither can the spirite of the defunct returne to his friend, or yet an Angell vse such formes.

PHI. And are not our war-woolfes one sorte of these spirits also, that hauntes and troubles some houses or dwelling places?

EPI. There bath indeede bene an old opinion of such like thinges; For by the Greekes they were called {Greek lukanðrwpoi} which signifieth men-woolfes. But to tell you simplie my opinion in this, if anie such thing hath bene, I take it to haue proceeded but of a naturall super-abundance of Melancholie, which as wee reade, that it hath made some thinke themselues Pitchers, and some horses, and some one kinde of beast or other: So suppose I that it hath so viciat the imagination and memorie of some, as per lucida interualla, it hath so highlie occupyed them, that they haue thought themselues verrie Woolfes indeede at these times: and so haue counterfeited their actiones in goeing on their handes and feete, preassing to deuoure women and barnes, fighting and snatching with all the towne dogges, and in vsing such like other bruitish actiones, and so to become beastes by a strong apprehension, as Nebucad-netzar was seuen yeares:[1] but as to their hauing and hyding of their hard & schellie sloughes, I take that to be but eiked, by vncertaine report, the author of all lyes.

---

[1] Dan. 4.

# CHAPTER II

## ARGV.

The description of the next two kindes of Spirites, whereof the one followes outwardlie, the other possesses inwardlie the persones that they trouble. That since all Prophecies and visiones are nowe ceased, all spirites that appeares in these formes are euill.

PHILOMATHES.

COme forward now to the reste of these kindes of spirites.

EPI. As to the next two kindes. that is, either these that outwardlie troubles and followes some persones, or else inwardlie possesses them: I will conjoyne them in one, because aswel the causes ar alike in the persons that they are permitted to trouble: as also the waies whereby they may be remedied and cured.

PHI. What kinde of persones are they that vses to be so troubled?

EPI. Two kindes in speciall: Either such as being guiltie of greeuous offences, God punishes by that horrible kinde of scourdge, or else being persones of the beste nature peraduenture, that yee shall finde in all the Countrie about them, G O D permittes them to be troubled in that sort, for the tryall of their patience, and wakening vp of their zeale, for admonishing of the beholders, not to truste ouer much in themselues, since they are made of no better stuffe, and peraduenture blotted with no smaller sinnes (as CHRIST saide, speaking of them vppon whome the Towre in Siloam fell:)[1] And for giuing likewise to the spectatators, matter to prayse G O D, that they meriting no better, are yet spared from being corrected in that fearefull forme.

PHI. These are good reasons for the parte of G O D, which apparantlie mooues him so to permit the Deuill to trouble such persones. But since the Deuil hath euer a contrarie respecte in all the actiones that G O D employes him in: which is I pray you the end and mark he shoots at in this turne?

EPI. It is to obtaine one of two thinges thereby, if he may: The one is the tinsell of their life, by inducing them to such perrilous places at such time as he either followes or possesses them, which may procure the same: And such like, so farre as G O D will permit him, by tormenting them to weaken their bodie, and caste them in incurable diseases. The other thing that hee preases to obteine by troubling of them, is the tinsell of their Soule, by intising them to mistruste and blaspheme God: Either for the intollerablenesse of their tormentes, as he assayed to haue done with IOB;[2] or else for his promising vnto them to leaue the troubling of them, incase they would so do, as is knowen by experience at this same time by the confession of a young one that was so troubled.

PHI. Since ye haue spoken now of both these kindes of spirites comprehending them in one: I must nowe goe backe againe in speering some questions of euerie one of these kindes in speciall. And first for these that followes certaine persones, yee know that there are two sortes of them: One sorte that troubles and tormentes the persones that they haunt with: An other sort that are seruiceable vnto them in all kinde of their necessaries, and omittes neuer to forwarne them of anie suddaine perrell that they are to be in. And so in this case, I would vnderstande whither both these sortes be but wicked and damned spirites: Or if the last sorte be rather Angells, (as should appeare by their actiones) sent

---

[1] Luc. 13.
[2] Iob. x.

by God to assist such as he speciallie fauoures. For it is written in the Scriptures, that God sendes Legions of Angells to guarde and watch ouer his elect.[1]

EPI. I know well inough where fra that errour which ye alleage hath proceeded: For it was the ignorant Gentiles that were the fountaine thereof. Who for that they knew not God, they forged in their owne imaginationes, euery man to be still accompanied with two spirites, whereof they called the one genius bonus, the other genius malus: the Greekes called them {Greek endaimona} & {Greek kakodaimona}: wherof the former they saide, perswaded him to all the good he did: the other entised him to all the euill. But praised be God we that are christians, & walks not amongst the Cymmerian conjectures of man, knowes well inough, that it is the good spirite of God onely, who is the fountain of all goodnes, that perswads vs to the thinking or doing of any good: and that it is our corrupted fleshe and Sathan, that intiseth vs to the contrarie. And yet the Deuill for confirming in the heades of ignoraunt Christians, that errour first mainteined among the Gentiles, he whiles among the first kinde of spirits that I speak of, appeared in time of Papistrie and blindnesse, and haunted diuers houses, without doing any euill, but doing as it were necessarie turnes vp and down the house: and this spirit they called Brownie in our language, who appeared like a rough-man: yea, some were so blinded, as to beleeue that their house was all the sonsier, as they called it, that such spirites resorted there.

PHI. But since the Deuils intention in all his actions. is euer to do euill,, what euill was there in that forme of doing, since their actions outwardly were good.

EPI Was it not euill inough to deceiue simple ignorantes, in making them to take him for an Angell of light, and so to account of Gods enemie, as of their particular friend: where by the contrarie, all we that are Christians, ought assuredly to know that since the comming of Christ in the flesh, and establishing of his Church by the Apostles, all miracles, visions, prophecies, & appearances of Angels or good spirites are ceased. Which serued onely for the first sowing of faith, & planting of the Church.

---

[1] Gen. 32. 1. Kin. 6 Psal. 34.

Where now the Church being established, and the white Horse whereof I spake before, hauing made his conqueste, the Lawe and Prophets are thought sufficient to serue vs, or make vs inexcusable, as Christ saith in his parable of Lazarus and the riche man.[1]

---

[1] Luk. 16.

# CHAPTER III

## ARGV.

The description of a particular sort of that kind of following spirites, called Incubi and Succubi: And what is the reason wherefore these kindes of spirites hauntes most the Northerne and barbarous partes of the world.

PHILOMATHES.

THE next question that I would speere, is likewise concerning this first of these two kindes of spirites that ye haue conjoyned: and it is this; ye knowe how it is commonly written and reported, that amongst the rest of the sortes of spirites that followes certaine persons, there is one more monstrous nor al the rest: in respect as it is alleaged, they converse naturally with them whom they trouble and hauntes with: and therefore I would knowe in two thinges your opinion herein: First if suche a thing can be: and next if it be: whether there be a difference of sexes amongst these spirites or not.

EPI. That abhominable kinde of the Deuils abusing of men or women, was called of old, Incubi and Succubi, according to the difference of the sexes that they conuersed with. By two meanes this great kinde of abuse might possibly be performed: The one, when the Deuill onelie as a spirite, and stealing out the sperme of a dead bodie, abuses them that way, they not graithlie seeing anie shape or feeling anie thing, but that which he so conuayes in that part: As we reade of a Monasterie of Nunnes which were burnt for their being that way abused. The other meane is when he borrowes a dead bodie and so visiblie, and as it seemes vnto them naturallie as a man converses with them. But it is to be noted, that in whatsoeuer way he vseth it, that sperme seemes intollerably cold to the person abused. For if he steale out the nature of a quick person, it cannot be so quicklie carryed, but it will both tine the strength and heate by the way, which it could neuer haue had for lacke of agitation, which in the time of procreation is the procurer & wakener vp of these two natural qualities. And if he occupying the dead bodie as his lodging expell the same out thereof in the dewe time, it must likewise be colde by the participation with the qualities of the dead bodie whereout of it comes. And whereas yee inquire if these spirites be diuided in sexes or not, I thinke the rules of Philosophie may easelie resolue a man of the contrarie: For it is a sure principle of that arte, that nothing can be diuided in sexes, except such liuing bodies as must haue a naturall seede to genere by. But we know spirites hath no seede proper to themselues, nor yet can they gender one with an other.

PHI. How is it then that they say sundrie monsters haue bene gotten by that way.

EPI. These tales are nothing but Aniles fabulæ. For that they haue no nature of their owne, I haue shewed you alreadie. And that the cold nature of a dead bodie, can woorke nothing in generation, it is more nor plaine, as being already dead of it selfe as well as the rest of the bodie is, wanting the naturall heate, and such other naturall operation, as is necessarie for woorking that effect, and incase such a thing were possible (which were all utterly against all the rules of nature) it would bread no monster, but onely such a naturall of-spring, as would haue cummed betuixt that man or woman and that other abused person, in-case they both being aliue had had a doe with other. For the Deuilles parte therein, is but the naked carrying or expelling of that substance: And so it coulde not participate with no qualitie of the same. Indeede, it is possible to the craft of the Deuill to make a womans bellie to swel after he hath that way abused her, which he may do, either by steiring vp her own humor, or by herbes, as we see beggars daily doe. And when the time of her deliuery should come to make her thoil great doloures, like vnto that naturall course, and then subtillie to slippe in the Mid-wiues handes, stockes, stones, or some monstruous barne brought from some other place, but this is more reported and gessed at by others, nor beleeued by me.

PHI. But what is the cause that this kinde of abuse is thought to be most common in such wild partes of the worlde, as Lap-land, and Fin-land, or in our North Iles of Orknay and Schet-land.

EPI. Because where the Deuill findes greatest ignorance and barbaritie, there assayles he grosseliest, as I gaue you the reason wherefore there was moe Witches of women kinde nor men.

PHI. Can anie be so vnhappie as to giue their willing consent to the Deuilles vilde abusing them in this forme.

EPI. Yea, some of the Witches haue confessed, that he hath perswaded them to giue their willing consent thereunto, that he may thereby haue them feltred the sikarer in his snares; But as the other compelled sorte is to be pittied and prayed for, so is this most highlie to be punished and detested.

PHI. It is not the thing which we cal the Mare, which takes folkes sleeping in their bedds, a kinde of these spirites, whereof ye are speaking?

EPI. No, that is but a naturall sicknes, which the Mediciners hath giuen that name of Incubus vnto ab incubando, because it being a thicke fleume, falling into our breast vpon the harte, while we are sleeping, intercludes so our vitall spirites, and takes all power from vs, as maks vs think that there were some vnnaturall burden or spirite, lying vpon vs and holding vs downe.

# CHAPTER IIII

## ARGV.

The description of the Dæmoniackes & possessed. By what reason the Papistes may haue power to cure them.

PHILOMATHES.

WEL, I haue told you now all my doubts, and ye haue satisfied me therein, concerning the first of these two kindes of spirites that ye haue conjoyned. Now I am to inquire onely two thinges at you concerning the last kinde, I meane the Dæmoniackes. The first is, whereby shal these possessed folks be discerned fra them that ar trubled with a natural Phrensie or Manie. The next is, how can it be that they can be remedied by the Papistes Church, whome wee counting as Hereticques, it should appeare that one Deuil should not cast out an other, for then would his kingdome be diuided in it selfe, as CHRIST said.[1]

EPI. As to your first question; there are diuers symptomes, whereby that heauie trouble may be discerned from a naturall sickenesse, and speciallie three, omitting the diuers vaine signes that the Papistes attributes vnto it: Such as the raging at holie water, their fleeing a back from the Croce, their not abiding the

---

[1] Mat. 12 Mark. 3

hearing of God named, and innumerable such like vaine thinges that were alike fashious and feckles to recite. But to come to these three symptomes then, whereof I spake, I account the one of them to be the incredible strength of the possessed creature, which will farre exceede the strength of six of the wightest and wodest of any other men that are not so troubled. The next is the boldning vp so far of the patients breast and bellie, with such an vnnaturall sturring and vehement agitation within them: And such an ironie hardnes of his sinnowes so stiffelie bended out, that it were not possible to prick out as it were the skinne of anie other person so far: so mightely works the Deuil in all the members and senses of his body, he being locallie within the same, suppose of his Soule and affections thereof, hee haue no more power then of any other mans. The last is, the speaking of sundrie languages, which the patient is knowen by them that were acquainte with him neuer to haue learned, and that with an vncouth and hollowe voice, and al the time of his speaking, a greater motion being in his breast then in his mouth. But fra this last symptome is excepted such, as are altogether in the time of their possessing bereft of al their senses being possessed with a dumme and blynde spirite, whereof Christ releiued one, in the 12. Of Mathew. And as to your next demande, it is first to be doubted if the Papistes or anie not professing the the onelie true Religion, can relieue anie of that trouble. And next, in-case they can, vpon what respectes it is possible vnto them. As to the former vpon two reasons, it is grounded: first that it is knowen so manie of them to bee counterfite, which wyle the Clergie inuentes for confirming of their rotten Religion. The next is, that by experience we finde that few, who are possessed indeede, are fullie cured by them: but rather the Deuill is content to release the bodelie hurting of them, for a shorte space, thereby to obteine the perpetual hurt of the soules of so many that by these false miracles may be induced or confirmed in the profession of that erroneous Religion: euen as I told you before that he doth in the false cures, or casting off of diseases by Witches. As to the other part of the argument in-case they can, which rather (with reuerence of the learned thinking otherwaies) I am induced to beleeue, by reason of the faithfull report that men sound of religion, haue made according to their sight thereof, I think if so be, I say these may be the respectes, whereupon the Papistes may haue that power. CHRIST gaue a commission and power to his Apostles to cast out Deuilles, which they according thereunto put in execution: The rules he had them obserue in that action, was fasting and praier: & the action it selfe to be done in his name. This power of theirs proceeded not then of anie vertue in them, but onely in him who directed them. As was clearly proued by Iudas his hauing as greate power in that commission, as anie of the reste. It is easie then to be vnderstand that the casting out of Deuilles, is by the vertue of fasting and prayer, and in-calling of the name of God, suppose manie imperfectiones be in the person that is the instrumente, as CHRIST him selfe teacheth vs of the power that false Prophets sall haue to caste out Devils.[1] It is no wounder then, these respects of this action being considered, that it may be possible to the Papistes, though erring in sundrie points of Religion to accomplish this, if they vse the right forme prescribed by CHRIST herein. For what the worse is that action that they erre in other thinges, more then their Baptisme is the worse that they erre in the other Sacrament, and haue eiked many vaine freittes to the Baptisme it selfe.

PHI. Surelie it is no little wonder that God should permit the bodies of anie of the faithfull to be so dishonoured, as to be a dwelling place to that vncleane spirite.

EPI. There is it which I told right now, would prooue and strengthen my argument of the deuils entring in the dead bodies of the faithfull. For if he is permitted to enter in their liuing bodies, euen when they are ioyned with the soule: how much more will God permit him to enter in their dead carions, which is no more man, but the filthie and corruptible caise of man. For as CHRIST Sayth, It is not any thing that enters within man that defiles him, but onely that which proceedes and commeth out of him.[2]

---

[1] Mat. 7.
[2] Mark. 7

# CHAPTER V

## ARGV.

The description of the fourth kinde of Spirites called the Phairie: What is possible therein, and what is but illusiones. How far this Dialogue entreates of all these thinges, and to what end.

PHILOMATHES.

NOW I pray you come on to that fourth kinde of spirites.

EPI. That fourth kinde of spirites, which by the Gentiles was called Diana, and her wandring Court, and amongst vs was called the Phairie (as I tould you) or our good neighboures, was one of the sortes of illusiones that was rifest in the time of Papistrie: for although it was holden odious to Prophesie by the deuill, yet whome these kinde of Spirites carryed awaie, and informed, they were thought to be sonsiest and of best life. To speake of the many vaine trattles founded vpon that illusion: How there was a King and Queene of Phairie, of such a iolly court & train as they had, how they had a teynd, & dutie, as it were, of all goods: how they naturallie rode and went, eate and drank, and did all other actiones like naturall men and women: I thinke it liker VIRGILS Campi Elysij, nor anie thing that ought to be beleeued by Christians, except in generall, that as I spake sundrie times before, the deuil illuded the senses of sundry simple creatures, in making them beleeue that they saw and harde such thinges as were nothing so indeed.

PHI. But how can it be then, that sundrie Witches haue gone to death with that confession, that they haue ben transported with the Phairie to such a hill, which opening, they went in, and there saw a faire Queene, who being now lighter, gaue them a stone that had sundrie vertues, which at sundrie times hath bene produced in judgement?

EPI. I say that, euen as I said before of that imaginar rauishing of the spirite foorth of the bodie. For may not the deuil object to their fantasie, their senses being dulled, and as it were a sleepe, such hilles & houses within them, such glistering courts and traines, and whatsoeuer such like wherewith he pleaseth to delude them. And in the meane time their bodies being senselesse, to conuay in their hande any stone or such like thing, which he makes them to imagine to haue receiued in such a place.

PHI. But what say ye to their fore-telling the death of sundrie persones, whome they alleage to haue seene in these places? That is, a sooth-dreame (as they say) since they see it walking.

EPI. I thinke that either they haue not bene sharply inough examined, that gaue so blunt a reason for their Prophesie, or otherwaies, I thinke it likewise as possible that the Deuill may prophesie to them when he deceiues their imaginationes in that sorte, as well as when he plainely speakes vnto them at other times for their prophesying, is but by a kinde of vision, as it were, wherein he commonly counterfeits God among the Ethnicks, as I told you before.

PHI. I would know now whether these kindes of spirites may only appeare to Witches, or if they may also appeare to anie other.

EPI. They may do to both, to the innocent sort, either to affraie them, or to seeme to be a better sorte of folkes nor vncleane spirites are, and to the Witches, to be a cullour of safetie for them, that ignorant Magistrates may not punish them for it, as I told euen now. But as the one sorte, for being perforce troubled with them ought to be pittied, so ought the other sorte (who may bee discerned by their taking vppon them to Prophesie by them,) That sorte I say, ought as seuerely to be punished as any other Witches, and rather the more, that that they goe dissemblingly to woorke.

PHI. And what makes the spirites haue so different names from others.

EPI. Euen the knauerie of that same deuil; who as hee illudes the Necromancers with innumerable feyned names for him and his angels, as in special, making Sathan, Beelzebub, & Lucifer, to be three sundry spirites, where we finde the two former, but diuers names giuen to the Prince of all the rebelling angels by the Scripture. As by CHRIST, the Prince of all the Deuilles is called, Beelzebub in that place, which I alleaged against the power of any hereticques to cast out Deuils. By IOHN in the Reuelation, the old tempter is called, Sathan the Prince of all the euill angels. And the last, to wit, Lucifer, is but by allegorie taken from the day Starre (so named in diuers places of the Scriptures) because of his excellencie (I meane the Prince of them) in his creation before his fall. Euen so I say he deceaues the Witches, by attributing to himselfe diuers names: as if euery diuers shape that he trans formes himselfe in, were a diuers kinde of spirit.

PHI. But I haue hard many moe strange tales of this Phairie, nor ye haue yet told me.

EPI. As well I do in that, as I did in all the rest of my discourse. For because the ground of this conference of ours, proceeded of your speering at me at our meeting, if there was such a thing as Witches or spirites: And if they had any power: I therefore haue framed my whole discours, only to proue that such things are and may be, by such number of examples as I show to be possible by reason: & keepes me from dipping any further in playing the part of a Dictionarie, to tell what euer I haue read or harde in that purpose, which both would exceede fayth, and rather would seeme to teach such vnlawfull artes, nor to disallow and condemne them, as it is the duetie of all Christians to do.

# CHAPTER VI

## ARGV.

Of the tryall and punishment of Witches. What sorte of accusation ought to be admitted against them. What is the cause of the increasing so far of their number in this age.

PHILOMATHES.

THEN To make an ende of our conference, since I see it drawes late, what forme of punishment thinke ye merites these Magicians and Witches? For I see that ye account them to be all alike guiltie?

EPI. They ought to be put to death according to the Law of God, the ciuill and imperial law, and municipall law of all Christian nations.

PHI. But what kinde of death I pray you?

EPI. It is commonly vsed by fire, but that is an indifferent thing to be vsed in euery cuntrie, according to the Law or custome thereof.

PHI. But ought no sexe, age nor ranck to be exempted?

EPI. None at al (being so vsed by the lawful Magistrate) for it is the highest poynt of Idolatrie, wherein no exception is admitted by the law of God.

PHI. Then bairnes may not be spared?

EPI. Yea, not a haire the lesse of my conclusion.

For they are not that capable of reason as to practise such thinges. And for any being in company and not reueiling thereof, their lesse and ignorant age will no doubt excuse them.

PHI. I see ye condemne them all that are of the counsell of such craftes.

EPI. No doubt, for as I said, speaking of Magie, the consulters, trusters in, ouer-seers, interteiners or sturrers vp of these craftes-folkes, are equallie guiltie with themselues that are the practisers.

PHI. Whether may the Prince then, or supreame Magistrate, spare or ouer-see any that are guiltie of that craft? vpon som great respects knowen to him?

EPI. The Prince or Magistrate for further tryals cause, may continue the punishing of them such a certaine space as he thinkes conuenient: But in the end to spare the life, and not to strike when God bids strike, and so seuerelie punish in so odious a fault & treason against God, it is not only vnlawful, but doubtlesse no lesse sinne in that Magistrate, nor it was in SAVLES sparing of AGAG[1]. And so comparable to the sin of Witch-craft it selfe, as SAMVELL alleaged at that time.

PHI. Surely then, I think since this crime ought to be so seuerely punished. Iudges ought to beware to condemne any, but such as they are sure are guiltie, neither should the clattering reporte of a carling serue in so weightie a case.

EPI. Iudges ought indeede to beware whome they condemne: For it is as great a crime (as SALOMON sayeth,) To condemne the innocent, as to let the guiltie escape free;[2] neither ought the

---

[1] 1. Sam. 15.
[2] Pro. 17

report of any one infamous person, be admitted for a sufficient proofe, which can stand of no law.

PHI. And what may a number then of guilty persons confessions, woork against one that is accused?

EPI. The assise must serue for interpretour of our law in that respect. But in my opinion, since in a mater of treason against the Prince, barnes or wiues, or neuer so diffamed persons, may of our law serue for sufficient witnesses and proofes. I thinke surely that by a far greater reason, such witnesses may be sufficient in matters of high treason against God: For who but Witches can be prooues, and so witnesses of the doings of Witches.

PHI. Indeed, I trow they wil be loath to put any honest man vpon their counsell. But what if they accuse folke to haue bene present at their Imaginar conuentiones in the spirite, when their bodies lyes sencelesse, as ye haue said.

EPI. I think they are not a haire the lesse guiltie: For the Deuill durst neuer haue borrowed their shaddow or similitude to that turne, if their consent had not bene at it: And the consent in these turnes is death of the law.

PHI. Then SAMVEL was a Witch: For the Deuill resembled his shape, and played his person in giuing response to SAVLE.

EPI. SAMVEL was dead aswell before that; and so none coulde slander him with medling in that vnlawfull arte. For the cause why, as I take it, that God will not permit Sathan to vse the shapes or similitudes of any innocent persones at such vnlawful times, is that God wil not permit that any innocent persons shalbe slandered with that vile defection: for then the deuil would find waies anew, to calumniate the best. And this we haue in proofe by them that are carryed with the Phairie, who neuer see the shaddowes of any in that courte, but of them that thereafter are tryed to haue bene brethren and sisters of that craft. And this was likewise proued by the co~fession of a young Lasse, troubled with spirites, laide on her by Witchcraft. That although shee saw the shapes of diuerse men & women troubling her, and naming the persons whom these shaddowes represents: yet neuer one of them are found to be innocent, but al clearely tried to be most guilty, & the most part of them confessing the same. And besides that, I think it hath ben seldome harde tell of, that any whome persones guiltie of that crime accused, as hauing knowen them to be their marrowes by eye-sight, and not by hear-say, but such as were so accused of Witch-craft. could not be clearely tryed vpon them, were at the least publickly knowen to be of a very euil life & reputation: so iealous is God I say, of the fame of them that are innocent in such causes. And besides that, there are two other good helpes that may be vsed for their trial: the one is the finding of their marke, and the trying the insensiblenes thereof. The other is their fleeting on the water: for as in a secret murther, if the deade carcase be at any time thereafter handled by the murtherer, it wil gush out of bloud, as if the blud wer crying to the heauen for reuenge of the murtherer. God hauing appoynted that secret super-naturall signe, for tryall of that secrete vnnaturall crime, so it appeares that God hath appoynted (for a super-naturall signe of the monstruous impietie of the Witches) that the water shal refuse to receiue them in her bosom, that haue shaken off them the sacred Water of Baptisme, and wilfullie refused the benefite thereof: No not so much as their eyes are able to shed teares (thretten and torture them as ye please) while first they repent (God not permitting them to dissemble their obstinacie in so horrible a crime) albeit the women kinde especially, be able otherwaies to shed teares at euery light occasion when they will, yea, although it were dissemblingly like the Crocodiles.

PHI. Well, wee haue made this conference to last as long as leasure would permit: And to conclude then, since I am to take my leaue of you, I pray God to purge this Cuntrie of these diuellishe practises: for they were neuer so rife in these partes, as they are now.

EPI. I pray God that so be to. But the causes ar ouer manifest, that makes them to be so rife. For the greate wickednesse of the people on the one parte, procures this horrible defection, whereby God justlie punisheth sinne, by a greater iniquitie. And on the other part, the consummation of the worlde, and our deliuerance drawing neare, makes Sathan to rage the more in his instruments, knowing his kingdome to be so neare an ende. And so fare-well for this time.[1]

**FINIS**

---

[1] Reuel. 2.